Tennis for
Young Champions

by Robert J. Antonacci
and Barbara D. Lockhart

Illustrations by Robert Handville

Tennis for Young Champions

McGraw-Hill Book Company
New York   St. Louis   San Francisco   Auckland   Bogotá
Hamburg   Johannesburg   London   Madrid   Mexico
Montreal   New Delhi   Panama   Paris   São Paulo
Singapore   Sydney   Tokyo   Toronto

123456789 BPBP 8765432

ISBN 0-07-002145-7

Library of Congress Cataloging in Publication Data

Antonacci, Robert Joseph, 1916–
    Tennis for young champions.

    Summary: Includes step-by-step instructions on racket grip, footwork, forehand, and backhand, as well as advice on serves, volleys, advanced strokes, doubles playing, and strategy.
    1. Tennis—Juvenile literature. [1. Tennis]
I. Lockhart, Barbara D. II. Handville, Robert, ill. III. Title.
GV996.5.A57   796.342′2   82–164
                                     AACR2
ISBN 0–07–002145–7

Contents

1

Tennis—The Great Court and Racket Game

"All set?"

The umpire sits on a high perch located at one end of the net. He is ready to start the tennis match. The players face one another as they stand at opposite ends of the court. Both are ready for play to start. It's Speedy Ron against Power Stroke Pete.

Bright lights flood the playing court of the huge indoor arena. Around the walls the stands are filled with boys and girls, men and women. They are tennis fans. Their eyes are on the server.

The umpire yells, "Players ready? Play!" Power Stroke Pete looks across the net and tosses the ball lightly into the air just above his head. Up goes the racket—and "whack!" The ball is hit over the net and onto the opponent's side of the court. The game is on!

Speedy Ron moves swiftly to his right and with a

quick racket motion returns the ball just over the net. Watch! Power Stroke Pete charges toward the net. Like a home-run slugger, he drives the ball hard across the net at a sharp angle. It appears that the ball is out of Speedy Ron's reach.

Look! Scrappy Ron looks beat! In the stands the crowd wonders. Will Speedy Ron get to the ball? Will he make the final arm stretch with his racket? Will he give up?

Without stopping, Ron whisks low and keeps on moving.

The crowd yells, "Stretch! Ron! Stretch! Smack the ball!"

As quick as lightning, Ron makes a last-ditch stretch with his racket, sending the ball skimming over the net and out of the reach of a surprised Pete.

This is modern tennis—the great racket game. How different today's exciting games of tennis are from the very early games that led to them.

TENNIS—THE EARLY YEARS

There are conflicting stories about when and where tennis had its beginning. Some historians believe that an early form of tennis was played by the ancient Egyptians and Arabs. Years later the Greeks and Romans copied the game. Each tennis was similar to the handball game of today with a single person hitting a crude ball against the wall with bare hands. Later, two players began to hit the ball back and forth.

RENAISSANCE PERIOD

During the thirteenth century in France, it was popular for the nobility, royalty, and clergy to play the *jeu de paume* or the "game of the palm." In Italy it was called *guioca della palla.*

These games were played in courtyards and monasteries with a flashy, awkward-looking ball stuffed with animal hair. Players "stroked" or "poked" the ball barehanded across a stretched rope, wooden barrier, or mound of dirt.

In time, the players started to use gloves, paddles, odd-shaped bats, and finally something that looked like a racket. These early games were known as *court tennis,* because they were first played in courtyards.

TENNIS GETS A NAME

How did tennis get its name? One version is that the game was named after an ancient city on the Nile in Egypt. The Arabs called it *tinnis,* and the Greeks named it *tanis.*

The most recent and popular explanation is that the origin of the word "tennis" is in the French command *tenez* ("hold"), which derives from the Latin *tenere.* The players shouted this word just before serving the ball.

Another story is told that the word "serve" is used in tennis because the earliest games were played mostly by royalty. A "servant" would receive the command to set the ball in motion to start the game.

TENNIS MOVES OUTDOORS

By the nineteenth century, only the wealthy were seen playing the game of tennis. The game caught on with the French. They took the popular game outdoors and called it *la longue paume.* At this time a cork ball made its first appearance. It had to be stroked or hit over a two-foot-high bank of dirt that served as a net. Players began to use rackets of a different shape, with wooden frames, handles, and gut strings.

The game later found its way to England, where it started to look more like the tennis of today.

FROM CROQUET LAWNS TO TENNIS LAWNS

There was an abundance of croquet lawns available throughout England. Along about 1860 the British were looking for new ways to use them.

It was in 1873 that a retired British major named Walter Clopton Wingfield first introduced a new outdoor game at a pheasant hunt. He called the game *sphairistike,* a name taken from the ancient Greek word meaning "to play." This new game soon became known as "tennis-on-the-lawn," and finally "lawn tennis." Major Wingfield patented the game in 1874.

The first lawn tennis game was played on a court shaped like an hourglass 60 feet long and 30 feet wide at the base lines. The court was divided by a net, which rose 7 feet high at the sidelines and sagged to 4 feet, 8 inches in the middle. The height of the net and shape of the court made the game slow and dull.

THE GAME SPEEDS UP

In 1875, the court was changed to the same length and width used in today's game. Another big change, made in 1882, was to lower the height of the net to 3 feet, 6 inches at the ends, and 3 feet at the center. These new rules called for players to use more speed, change-of-direction and stop-and-go running, and stroking accuracy.

THE BERMUDA VACATION

It was chiefly members of the British military who were responsible for introducing lawn tennis to other parts of the world. In Bermuda some soldiers made plans to give a demonstration of how the game was played. An American woman visiting the island was among the guests invited to watch the demonstration.

The American woman watched. Took notes. And liked the action. She even convinced the British soldiers to lend her some equipment to take back to America. She was Mary Ewing Outerbridge, who is now often called the "great-great-grandmother of American tennis." In March 1874, she began to pack to return home to Staten Island, New York. She ran into difficulty with the customs officials before they allowed her to take the tennis equipment back to America with her.

LAWN TENNIS ARRIVES IN AMERICA

When Miss Outerbridge arrived home, she prepared to introduce the game to her friends. In

1874, she got permission to build a court on the edge of the Staten Island Cricket and Baseball Club field. It was the first lawn tennis court in America.

She demonstrated the game to a group of women friends, who at first were not sure whether it was ladylike to go after a ball and stroke it over a net. But with the help of Miss Outerbridge's brothers, who were also members of the Cricket Club, the game soon began to catch on.

OFFICIAL RULES ARE ADOPTED

In 1881, the United States Lawn Tennis Association was organized. The new association established all the rules of the game. It decided what the sizes of the ball, racket, and court must be, and how to score the game. In 1975, it changed its name to the United States Tennis Association (USTA) because very few lawn-tennis courts remained.

Another large organization is The International Tennis Federation. It started in England in 1913 as the International Lawn Tennis Federation. This group dictates the rules that must be followed in competition between different nations.

EARLY UNIFORMS

There were no specific uniforms or dresses required of the early tennis players. Men generally wore long pants, long-sleeved shirt and jacket, silk ascot, and sometimes, a top hat. Women wore layers upon layers of clothes that even covered

FIRST "BIG" TOURNAMENT IN U.S.A.,
STATEN ISLAND, 1880

their shoes. You can see why the players, at first, had a difficult time reaching for a ball.

There are many accounts of women tripping over their long skirts while they tried to stretch for a low ball. The main idea was for players to be graceful when they hit the ball over the net, not for them to return it, necessarily.

The invention of the overhead serve speeded up the play. The rules changed and now required men and women to wear all-white clothing. Men wore light, long pants and a shirt, while women wore fewer layers of clothing, with their skirts raised to just above the ankle.

As the action of the game improved so did the

rules for the tennis player's dress. Tennis shorts first appeared at the U.S. National Championships at Forest Hills, New York, in 1932. Today, men, women, boys, and girls wear different styles of shorts or skirts, and shirts that are fashionable and comfortable. Many women wear short, one-piece dresses.

EARLY RACKETS

The shape of the early tennis rackets in America was more square than oval. Heavy-gauge gut was strung loosely to the one-piece frames of ash wood The loose gut had players using a "push" or "peck" stroke to get the ball over the net, instead of a free-striking motion.

Around 1928, the laminated hickory and beech-wood frame appeared on the market. The gut of the racket was of a fine grade and tightly stretched to the frame. Play action speeded up, and the ball traveled faster once it made contact with the racket. Today's models are made of sleek, top-grade wood, fiber glass, steel, aluminum, and graphite.

CHAMPIONSHIP PLAY STILL GOING STRONG

Probably the most popular tennis tournament in the world is at *Wimbledon* (the British National Championship). It originated in England in 1877 and was named after the London suburb where the action takes place every year. The *All-England Club* had a lot of influence on the game at this time.

One of its first notices, pinned on the bulletin board of its newly-constructed facilities on July 24, 1868, read: "Gentlemen are requested not to play in their shirtsleeves when ladies are present." During this same period, it also was improper for a lady to get her layers of clothing soiled or to be seen to perspire.

The first *United States Nationals* were held for men's singles and doubles in 1881. The first women's singles championships were held in 1887, and in 1890 for doubles play. They were played at Newport, Rhode Island; Forest Hills, New York; Philadelphia; back to Forest Hills; and finally, since 1978, at Flushing Meadow, New York. Since 1968, the tournament has been called the *U.S. Open Tennis Championships*.

The annual *Davis Cup* matches began in 1900 as a competition between the best male players from England and the United States. The "cup" was named after Dwight Davis, a wealthy Harvard student who donated one thousand dollars for the first cup. After 1904, other countries became participants in the tournament.

The yearly *Wightman Cup* competition started in 1923 as a dual meet between the United States and British women's teams. The cup is named after Hazel H. Wightman, who won many championships between 1909 and 1920.

MORE CHAMPIONSHIP PLAY

Many countries sponsor their own tournaments, all of them trying to attract players from all over the world. Some of the most popular are the Australian, French, and Italian Open Tennis Tournaments.

TENNIS AN OLYMPIC SPORT

The amateur sport of tennis spread rapidly throughout the world. It was adopted as a sport in the World Olympic Games in 1896 and dropped after the 1924 Games because officials believed there were too many sports on the program. However, the International Olympic Committee (IOC) voted to include tennis once again as an event beginning with the summer Olympic Games in 1988, which will be held in Seoul, South Korea.

OPEN COMPETITION BEGINS

Practically all the major world and American Championship tournaments are now *open* for amateurs and professionals to compete against one another. The Wimbledon and the U.S. Nationals were the first to allow open competition in 1968. New organizations quickly began to sponsor their own world and national tournaments. Many of these tournaments are covered on TV and radio, and in newspapers and magazines. The athletes are paid to play and receive large amounts of money when they win.

"GRAND SLAM" OF TENNIS

Players winning the United States, Australian,

French, and Wimbledon Open Championships in the same year are known as winners of the "Grand Slam" of tennis. The first man to achieve the honor was an American, Don Budge, in 1938. The first woman to accomplish the feat was also an American, Maureen "Little Mo" Connelly, in 1953.

PRESIDENTS AND TENNIS

Theodore Roosevelt, the 26th President, *Woodrow Wilson,* the 28th, and *Warren G. Harding,* the 29th, all tried to play a little tennis. Teddy Roosevelt always favored fast action and more vigorous activities. He found tennis too slow and decided to spend his time in other recreational sports. Teddy would have loved today's game, which calls for speed, agility and stamina! The racket Woodrow Wilson used can be seen in the permanent collection on the history of sports in America at the Smithsonian Institution in Washington, D.C.

John F. Kennedy, the 35th President, was probably the most active games player of all the Presidents. His family properties always included large recreational sports areas. This made it easy for family members and friends to compete in many different events. Among the many sports Kennedy played was tennis. He was quite good at it. When he felt like a game of singles or doubles, there were always enough Kennedys or guests around to start a game.

Gerald R. Ford, 38th President, who is considered to be one of the most talented athletes of all the Presidents, has found more time for tennis since leaving office. He continues to play an occasional game for exercise and in "celebrity" tournaments to raise money for charity.

Jimmy Carter, the 39th President, and his wife, Rosalynn, played tennis on the White House and Camp David courts whenever they found time.

ONE-HUNDREDTH ANNIVERSARY

Recognizing tennis as a great sport, the United States Post Office in 1974 issued a special ten-cent commemorative envelope to celebrate the one-hundredth anniversary of the game in America.

The *Tennis Hall of Fame and Museum* was dedicated in Newport Casino (meaning "little house") in Newport, Rhode Island, where the game had its early beginnings. Thousands of people visit this museum every year. In it are pictures, equipment, and other materials used by the great players of the past and the early founders of tennis.

MORE TENNIS HISTORY

James Dwight, who played lawn tennis as early as 1875 when it was still known as *sphairistike,* is known as the "Father of American Tennis." He won several U.S. National titles and headed the U.S. Lawn Tennis Association for twenty-one years.

Hazel H. Wightman, winner of many tennis titles from 1909 to 1920, is known as the "Queen Mother of American Tennis."

Althea Gibson was the first black ever to play in a major tennis tournament. She competed in the 1950 U.S. Nationals. She did not win, but she later won several of the major American and world tennis championships.

Arthur Ashe was the first black male to win a major tennis title. He won the first U.S. Open Tennis Championships in 1968.

The greatest number of games in an official tournament singles match is 126! It happened in 1966, in the King's Cup Tennis Play competition, when a British player beat his Polish opponent 27–29, 31–29, 6–4 in a match that lasted over four and one-half hours.

SCHOOL AND COLLEGE PLAY

The National Collegiate Athletic Association (NCAA) sponsors tournaments for college men, while the women's competition is organized by the Association of Intercollegiate Athletics for Women (AIAW). Boys' and girls' tennis meets are sponsored by the National Federation of High School Associations (NFHSA). These associations all follow the rules of the United States Tennis Association, which also prepares contests for the different age groups.

BOYS' AND GIRLS' COMPETITION

Did you know that tennis competitions for young people are very popular in the United States? The

United States Tennis Association and elementary schools have developed special rules for young girls and boys who wish to take part in tennis competition. City recreation departments, the YM/YWCA, camps, Boy Scouts, Girl Scouts, CYO, and neighborhood clubs also sponsor contests for youngsters.

Later on in this book you will learn more about the different programs that youngsters can participate in for championships. You will also learn how to train and improve your tennis skills so you will enjoy the game more.

2

Know Your Tennis

Tennis is exciting! It's fun to play this game, watch it, and read about it. Whether you are a player or a fan, you will enjoy tennis much more when you know the rules and understand the fine points.

Keep a *tennis notebook.* Write the most important rules in it. Put down other information you learn. See how well you can keep score and predict the winners of a match. After you get to know tennis, no doubt you will qualify as an amateur coach and will be able to tell people how to play the game.

IDEA OF THE GAME

Tennis is a game that is played on an indoor or outdoor hard-surface court that is divided in the middle by a net. It is played between two players (singles game) or four players (doubles game) with rackets and a ball. The game begins when one of the players puts the ball into play with an overhand serve. The ball must travel over the net and into the opposite service-court area. The ball is then hit back and forth over the net until a player misses it, or until it lands outside the court boundary lines or fails to clear the net.

THE TENNIS COURT

Did you know that the size of the court is different for the singles and doubles game? The tennis-playing area is called a *court*. It is rectangular in shape.

The *singles court* is 78 feet long and 27 feet wide. The net that divides the court in the middle measures 3 feet 6 inches high at the posts and 3 feet high at the exact center.

The side boundary lines are called the *singles sidelines*, and the end boundary lines are known as the *base lines*. Another line 21 feet away from each side of the net is connected with the sidelines. These are called the *service lines*.

The space on each side of the net between the two service lines and the sidelines is divided into four equal parts. This is shown by a line running down the length of the court, which connects the very center of each service line. This line is named the *center-service line*. The four spaces (two on each side of the net) are known as the *service courts*. The areas between the base lines and the service lines are called the *backcourts*. The 4-inch

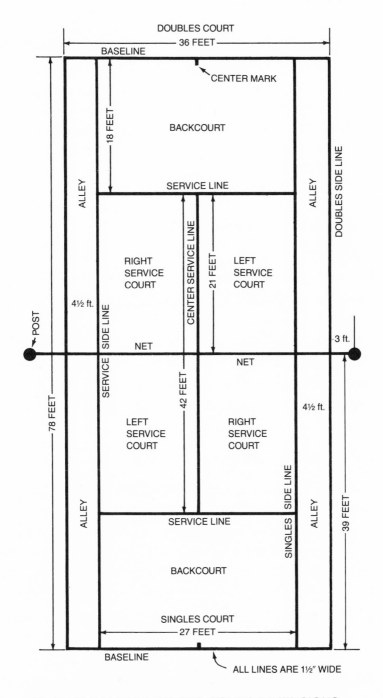

DOUBLES COURT
36 FEET
BASELINE
CENTER MARK
18 FEET
BACKCOURT
SERVICE LINE
ALLEY
DOUBLES SIDE LINE
CENTER SERVICE LINE
RIGHT SERVICE COURT
21 FEET
LEFT SERVICE COURT
4½ ft.
SERVICE SIDE LINE
POST
NET
NET
3 ft.
78 FEET
42 FEET
LEFT SERVICE COURT
RIGHT SERVICE COURT
4½ ft.
SINGLES SIDE LINE
ALLEY
SERVICE LINE
39 FEET
BACKCOURT
SINGLES COURT
27 FEET
BASELINE
ALL LINES ARE 1½" WIDE

SINGLES-DOUBLES TENNIS COURT DIMENSIONS

marks located at the exact center of each base line inside the court area are called the *center marks*.

When you play doubles, the width of the playing area is increased by adding a *doubles sideline* 54 inches from each of the singles sidelines. The spaces between the singles and doubles sidelines are called the *alleys*.

THE SERVER AND RECEIVER

In singles, two players stand on opposite sides of the net. The player who hits the ball to start the game is called the *server*. The other player, the opponent, is the *receiver*. The server continues to serve until a game is won by one of the players. After each game the server becomes the receiver and the receiver the server. This exchange goes on until one of the players wins the total match.

WHO SERVES FIRST?

A toss of a coin in the air decides which player will serve first. The winner of the toss may choose to serve or receive. The loser chooses the side of the court from which to receive. Players without a coin often spin the racket head on the ground. As with the coin toss, the winner's side is up.

A "SERVICE" STARTS THE GAME

Play always begins with a serve from the right side of the court. Both of the server's feet must be behind the base line and between the center marker and right sideline. The ball is tossed into the air and struck before it drops to the ground.

A LEGAL SERVE

The service stroke must be made with the racket meeting the ball before either foot goes over or touches the base line. The served ball must travel over the net and land within the opponent's right-side service court. The opponent must let the ball bounce once before returning it back over the net to the server's side of the court.

CHANGE COURT POSITION AFTER EVERY POINT

After the first point of the game, both the server and receiver move to positions on their own left side of the service court. The change from the right service court to the left and back to the right goes on after every point until the end of the game.

CHANGING COURT SIDES AFTER GAME

Players must change court sides after the end of odd-numbered games or as agreed upon by opponents before play begins. The players go to their opposite sides of the court at the end of the first game and after every two games that follow. If a set ends in an even number of games, the change of court side is not made until the end of the first game of the next set.

THE SERVER'S "FAULTS!"

The server has two chances to serve the ball within the opponent's service court. If the ball does not land in the opponent's service court, it becomes known as a *fault*. A point is scored for the receiver when *two faults* are made in a row. The server makes a fault in the following ways:

1. By missing the ball completely after tossing it into the air for a service stroke.
2. By failing to hit the ball within the opponent's court.
3. By serving the ball into the net.
4. After the ball is served, it hits the net post.
5. After the ball is served, it hits a doubles partner before going over the net.

The following are also server's faults, but they are better known as *foot faults:*

1. The server steps on or over the base line *before* striking the ball on the serve.
2. The server takes a walking or running start just before hitting the ball.
3. The server hits the ball from outside the serving area between the center marker and sideline.

A "LET" SERVICE

When a serve ball hits the top of the net and lands in the opponent's correct service court, the serve is called a *let service*. This means that there is no penalty for the stroke. The server gets another chance to make a good serve. It is also a *let* when the ball is served before the receiver is in ready position to play. When this happens the server must try the play over again.

RETURNING THE SERVE

The receiver of the serve must allow the ball to bounce once inside the service-court area before trying a return shot. When this rule is not obeyed, a point is awarded to the server. After a legal serve is returned, either player has the choice of hitting the ball "on the fly" (volleying) or after the first bounce.

HOW POINTS ARE LOST

"Losing a point" really means that a point is awarded to the opponent. There are several ways a player can lose points. The most important rules are:

1. If a player hits the ball more than once in an attempt to get the ball over the net in one stroke, the opponent receives a point. This if often called a *double hit*.
2. Any player who hits the ball before it passes over his or her side of the net loses a point.
3. A point is lost if a player throws the racket to strike the ball.

4. A point is lost when the server makes two faults.
5. If a player's racket or clothing touches the net while the ball is in play, a point is awarded to the opponent.
6. If a player's body or clothing is touched by a ball in play, a point is awarded to the opponent.
7. A point is awarded to the opponent if a player does not return the ball before the second bounce.
8. A point is lost when a player fails to return the ball within the boundary of the opponent's side of the court.

SPECIAL RULES ON RETURN STROKES

There are some interesting rules that must be remembered by all tennis players. Did you know that it's legal to hit a ball from outside the court boundaries? As long as the ball is hit on the fly or in the air before it touches the ground, the ball is legally in play. Of course, the return hit ball must go over the net and land within the opponent's side of the court.

The ball is also in play when it hits into the net or post and lands over the net and into the opponent's side of the court. A ball that hits any part of the boundary lines is legally in play. After a player hits the ball on a legal return stroke, his or her racket is allowed to pass over the net. Of course, no part of the player's clothing or racket must touch the net on this play.

THE DOUBLES SERVE

In the *doubles game,* two players form a team to play partners against two other players. The four service areas remain the same, but the court playing area is widened. The game is scored the same as in singles, and the serve changes sides after every game.

The teams decide which player will serve first for their side. Each player serves after every fourth game. When a player in doubles serves from the right side of the court, the partner usually stands ready closer to the net on the left side of the court. When one player serves from the left side of the court, the partner shifts to the front-right side of the court.

RECEIVING THE DOUBLES SERVE

At the beginning of the doubles game the two players receiving the serve decide which service court they will play. The player receiving the first serve continues to receive the serve on that court throughout the whole *set* (six or more games). This player is free to run and play anywhere on the court after the return. The other partner will receive all the serves hit on the other service court.

The scoring in a tennis game is somewhat different from most other games. The server's score is always given first even if it is lower than that of the opponent. Instead of 1, 2, 3, etc., points are awarded as follows:

- Zero (0) score is called "love"
- First point is called "15"
- Second point is called "30"
- Third point is called "40"
- The winning (next) point is called "game"

Here is an example of scoring a game. If the server wins the first point, the score is 15 (server)–love (receiver). If the receiver wins the next point, the score would be 15–15, or 15–all. If the next point is won by the server, the score becomes 30–15. Another point is won by the server and the score becomes 40–15. Another point is finally won by the receiver and the score becomes 40–30. The next point (the server's fourth) is won by the server for a final winning score of "game."

The first player to make four points wins the game. However, the winning player must beat the opponent by two or more points. In the above example the server was winning 40–30 and won the next (fourth) point to win the game by at least two points.

If the opponent had won that point, the score would have been 40–40. This score is known as *deuce* (a tie), which means that each player has won three points. When players are tied at 40–40, one must make two more points in a row to win the game. If the server wins the next point after a deuce, it is the server's *advantage* or *ad,* and the score is called *ad in.* If the server also wins the very next point, it is *game.* However, if the receiver wins the point after a 40–40 (deuce), the receiver gets the advantage and the score is called *ad out.* If the receiver also wins the next point, the receiver wins the game.

MORE PRACTICE KEEPING SCORE

Let's keep score for a make-believe game. You are the server.

THE SERVER WINS:	THE RECEIVER WINS:		THE SCORE IS:
1st point	zero points	=	15 — love
2nd point	zero points	=	30 — love
zero points	1st point	=	30 — 15
3rd point	zero points	=	40 — 15
zero points	2nd point	=	40 — 30
4th point	zero points	=	game (server)

Here is another game with two players who are very close in playing ability.

THE SERVER WINS:	THE RECEIVER WINS:		THE SCORE IS:
1st point	zero points	=	15 — love
2nd point	zero points	=	30 — love
zero points	1st point	=	30 — 15
zero points	2nd point	=	30 — 30 (all)
zero points	3rd point	=	30 — 40 (ad out)

3rd point	zero points	=	40 — 40 (deuce)
4th point	zero points	=	ad in (server)
zero points	5th point	=	deuce (tie)
zero points	6th point	=	ad out (receiver)
zero points	7th point	=	game (receiver)

WINNING A SET

The first player or doubles team to win six games wins what is known as a *set*. However, you must win the set by two games or win the tiebreaker. If the players get to a 5–5 game tie, the set continues until one of the players wins two games in a row. The final set score would be 7–5, 8–6, 9–7, 10–8, and so on. In other words, you cannot win the set by a score of 6–5.

Tiebreaker rule. If the game score is 6–all, you may play the *tiebreaker* instead of playing until someone wins two games in a row. This scoring system allows you to determine the winner of the set without playing additional games. There is a *9-point* sudden-death tiebreaker and a *12-point* sudden-death tiebreaker and a 12-point sudden-death tiebreaker rule. The first player to win 5 points in the 9-point tiebreaker wins the set 7 games to 6. Coaches and tournament officials usually decide if a tiebreaker rule will be used during the competition.

WINNING A MATCH

In *men's* championship play, the first player or

team to win three out of five sets wins the match. For *women's* play, the first to win two out of three sets wins the match. For boys and girls sixteen years of age and younger the first to win two out of three sets wins the match. A ten-minute rest is often given between the third and fourth set for men. Younger players usually have a ten-minute rest between the second and third sets.

EQUIPMENT

There are two kinds of equipment for the game of tennis. They are the *field* or *permanent equipment* and the *personal equipment.*

The *field equipment* includes the posts, the net, the metal cable or cord, backstops and sidestops to keep the ball from going into the spectator areas, the officials' stands and chairs surrounding the court, and the spectator stands.

The *personal equipment* or supplies include the racket, balls, athletic socks, and sneakers with rubber soles. The clothing worn by the players comes in many different styles. Most girls wear tennis dresses or shorts and a top, while boys wear shorts and T-shirts. Some players also wear head- and wristbands, and sometimes knee, ankle, and elbow supports for temporary physical problems.

THE RACKET

Tennis rackets come in different weights and different handle-grip sizes. Check with a well-known

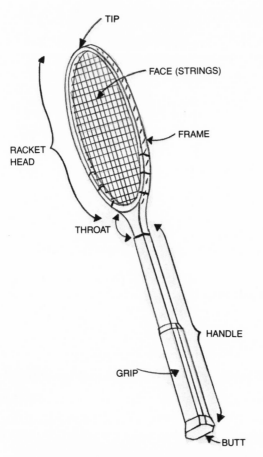

TIP

FACE (STRINGS)

FRAME

RACKET
HEAD

THROAT

HANDLE

GRIP

BUTT

sporting-goods store or with a teacher to find the best weight and handle for you.

Each portion of the racket has a name. The section where you grip the racket is called the *handle* or *grip*. The end of the handle is called the *butt* or *heel*. The portion that joins the handle and the frame of the strings is the *throat*. The strings of the racket are also known as the *racket face,* and the frame surrounding the strings is known as the *racket head*. The very top of the racket head is the *tip*.

DIFFERENT GROUP COMPETITIONS

The United States Tennis Association (USTA) and its local branches sponsor tournaments for many different age groups. There is competition for players ten years of age and under, twelve years and under, fourteen years and under, sixteen and under, eighteen and under, twenty-one and under, and an open division for all players. There are also separate competitions for men and women only.

MORE TENNIS EVENTS

The types of events sponsored most often are the following:

1. Men's singles and doubles play
2. Women's singles and doubles play
3. Mixed doubles (one man and one woman on a team)
4. Husband-and-wife mixed doubles team
5. Father-and-son doubles team
6. Mother-and-daughter doubles team
7. Brother-and-sister mixed doubles team

Now that you know more about the game of tennis, your next job is to learn how to play the game.

3

Racket Grip and Footwork —Let's Get Started!

From the time the umpire gives the command to "begin play" until the end of the game, tennis players keep on the move.

Players move at full speed. They make quick, running steps. They shift and pivot. They need good footwork to move toward the right position to meet the ball. These speedy moves are all made while the player keeps a grip on the racket. Smart footwork and a good racket grip help you to play a better game.

A successful player and coach once said, "Before you actually start to play tennis, think of yourself as a tennis player. When you go out onto the court, move your body *thinking* of yourself as a player. Don't just think of yourself as a person only 'trying out tennis.' Think Tennis! Say *'I am a tennis player.'* Then start moving like one on the court."

Let's get started by learning how to hold the racket.

GRIPPING THE RACKET

Different grips are used for different strokes. Learn and practice the most popular ones at first. As you grow stronger and your game improves, you may be ready to try a new grip. The three most popular grips used throughout the world are:

1. Forehand (Eastern) grip
2. Backhand (Continental) grip
3. Two-handed grip

THE FOREHAND GRIP

The most popular *forehand grip* is the *Eastern grip*. It is used to make a forehand stroke at balls that are traveling toward the racket side of your body. This is what you do to take the forehand grip. Have the tip of the racket frame touch the ground slightly in front of your feet so it is pointing forward and back. Keep the racket steady by placing your free hand around the throat of the racket.

1. Grip or pick up the handle with your racket hand as if you were "shaking hands" with the racket.
2. You are holding the racket in the center of the hand grip so the "butt end" of the handle sticks out just a little beyond the heel of your hand.
3. Notice how your thumb and first finger have formed a "V" shape. The V should be pointing down the middle of the handle toward the throat of the racket.
4. Your fingers are slightly spread and

RIGHT HAND
FOREHAND GRIP

NORTH

SOUTH

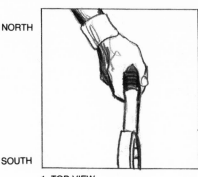

1. TOP VIEW

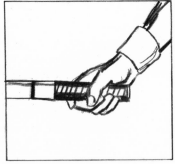

2. FRONT VIEW

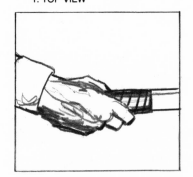

3. REAR VIEW

wrapped well around the handle. The *first finger* is farther away from the others in a position that makes it look like a "trigger" finger. This completes the forehand grip.

How does the grip feel? Does it feel comfortable? Do you notice the position of the racket slanted a little *upward?*

It's very important that you work on these fine points now, because they will be *crucial* to the success of your forehand drive later. Mastering these points early will get you in the habit of always having your wrist ready and cocked slightly higher than the forearm when it's needed in a game. Learning this rule helps to make sure that you *keep that racket up!*

RIGHT HAND
BACKHAND GRIP

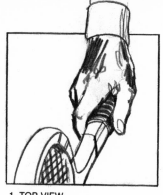

1. TOP VIEW

2. FRONT VIEW

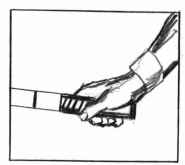

3. REAR VIEW

THE BACKHAND GRIP

The *Continental* grip is almost always used to make a *backhand* stroke. It is used when the ball travels toward the free side (opposite the racket side) of your body. Take a loose forehand grip on the handle with your racket hand. Hold the throat portion of the racket firmly with your other hand.

1. Twist or rotate the racket hand one-quarter turn inward toward the other arm. The palm is now more on top of the handle. The shape of the V points toward the throat of the racket and along the upper-inside corner of the handle.
2. The large knuckle of the first finger should

33

be over the upper-inside corner of the handle.

3. Your fingers are spread so they feel comfortable, and with the first finger farther apart you create the "trigger" position that you used in the forehand grip.

4. Keep the *racket head up* at all times. And keep supporting the throat portion of the racket with your left hand—until you are ready to hit the backhand stroke.

TWO-HANDED GRIP

The *two-handed grip* allows you to have more power and better control of the racket than the one-handed grip. However, the two-handed grip will not let you stretch or reach for a ball as far as the one-handed grip does.

The Two-Handed Backhand Grip. Hold a racket with both your hands.

1. Take a regular backhand grip with your racket hand just as you were taught earlier.

TWO-HAND BACKHAND GRIP
—RIGHT HAND PLAYER

2. Place your other hand directly above your racket hand with a forehand grip.
3. You now have a *two-handed backhand grip.* It gets you ready to make a two-handed backhand stroke.

The Two-Handed Forehand Grip. This is what you do.

1. Take a regular forehand grip with your racket hand.
2. Take a backhand grip with the free hand directly above the racket hand.
3. You have completed the *two-handed forehand grip.* You are ready for a two-handed forehand stroke.

Here are additional pointers to help you with the grips. Don't wear out your forearm by holding the racket too tightly throughout the whole game. Hold the racket *firmly* when you're hitting. *Relax* the grip when you're not hitting. Don't let the racket head drop when you are using the racket. Keep the racket head up. If you think the head must be lowered to meet the ball, get your body lower by *bending your knees* and stretching your forearms. Never let your wrists droop. Keep them firm or cocked throughout your stroke.

THE STANCE—YOUR "READY POSITION"

After you have practiced the different grips, you will need to learn how to get your racket to where

TWO STANCES—YOUR "READY POSITION"

the opponent has hit the ball. Games are often won and lost on *how well a player can move swiftly* from one area of the court to another.

A good *stance* gets you in a *ready position* to move swiftly into any play that may take place. Here is what you do:

1. Pretend you are standing at the base line, facing the net. Take your regular forehand grip on the racket. Place your free hand at the throat, and support the weight of the racket on your fingertips.
2. Have your feet shoulder-width apart with your toes pointing straight ahead. Knees are

bent as if you were going to sit down halfway.

3. Keep your upper body straight, and lean slightly forward over your knees and legs. Your weight is now on the balls of your feet.

4. Your arms are held a little in front of you so that the elbow of the racket hand is over the racket-side knee. The other elbow is a trifle more in front.

5. Get the racket head pointing up and toward the net with the frame facing up and down, and the face parallel to the sidelines. Keep your head up and your eyes looking over the net to get a clear view of your opponent, ball, or a teammate when you play doubles.

This is your tennis player's stance. It will help you to move into a *ready hitting position* for any ball that your opponent sends over the net.

Here are some additional tips to help you get started.

1. Get into your *ready stance.*

2. Bounce lightly on your feet by raising the weight of your body off your heels and onto the balls of your feet. Be ready to move with speed in any direction.

3. *Don't get caught flat-footed.* In other words, never stand with all your body weight resting on all parts of your feet, relaxed as you are when talking to a friend. Do this only when the ball is not in play.

4. Be sure to bend your knees! Stay low!

Practice getting into this position over and over until it feels natural. You should feel comfortable, relaxed, and alert in the *ready* position. You should also start looking like a tennis player!

SMART FOOTWORK

Fans like to see a tennis player with good footwork. These players move forward, backward, and sideways with speed. Young players know it's more fun to be able to get the racket into position in time to hit the opponent's ball.

Do you want to move swiftly toward a ball hit near you? Away from you? Would you like to learn how to make those *first starts* with a "slide" or "shuffle," or "pivot" step? This is the way you do it.

Quick Sideways Moves. Take a ready position by starting with a forehand grip on the racket. Have the free hand support the racket at the throat. Keep the racket *head up.* Loosen up and stay alert by bouncing lightly onto the balls of your feet.

1. Move sideways swiftly to the racket side of your body by pushing off with the other foot. Make your first sliding-step motion with the racket-side foot.
2. Quickly slide the free-side foot toward the racket-side foot. Push off again with the free foot and make another sideward slide with the racket foot. Get the opposite (free-side) foot to slide toward the racket-side foot once again.

3. Move toward the opposite direction to get back where you started. This time, push off hard with the racket foot, and start your sideward slide with the free-side foot. Make two complete sideward slide steps until you reach the spot where you began. That's all there is to it.

Were you always in a ready position throughout the sideways shifting? Were you always facing forward? Were you holding your racket correctly? Did you notice that your footwork was similar to a guard's movements in basketball?

Go through these moves once more. This time increase your distance and speed by making five slides to the racket side of your body and five slide steps back toward the other side.

Every time you work on these moves, check to see if you are making the slides, or shuffle steps, smoothly. Are the knees always bent with little or no up-and-down motion of the head and body? Are you ready to change your racket grip in a hurry?

When you begin moving to reach an imaginary ball on your racket side, quickly take a forehand grip to stroke the ball. To reach balls traveling on the opposite side, be ready to shift quickly to a backhand grip.

FRONT PIVOT STEPS—MOVING TOWARD THE BALL

You have already learned about the different grips, the ready position, and how to move from one side of the court to the other. You are now ready to learn how to move your body into the best position to hit the ball.

The best way to prepare to hit the ball is by using a *pivot step*. A pivot is a type of turn. All tennis players use the pivot step because it helps them move into the correct position to hit the ball without wasting time. To make a pivot for a forehand shot:

1. Take a forehand grip and get into the ready position. Make two slide or shuffle steps to your racket side. Slide the racket-side foot once more toward the same side. This becomes your *pivot* foot.

2. Quickly take your weight off the heel of the pivot foot and turn (pivot) forward and inward on the ball of your foot. Always keep the ball of the pivot foot on the ground. Your body makes a quarter-turn inward as you make the pivot. Let the free-side foot follow the direction of the quarter-turn so it lands forward and to the side about a foot from the pivot foot.

3. With a push-off from the pivot foot, most of your body weight is shifted to the front foot. Your free-side shoulder and hip are now turned toward the net. The front foot is "opened" to a forty-five degree angle, with your toe pointing toward the net post facing you. The toe of the racket foot is pointing straight toward the sideline.

Here is how you make the *pivot for a backhand*

stroke. Make the same moves with the free side of your body that you just made with your racket side. The foot opposite the racket side becomes the pivot foot, and the racket-side foot is forward in an open position facing the net.

More Pivoting. Try the pivot movements again with the forehand and backhand grips. Repeat each of these pivots about five times. Always start at the beginning by taking the regular ready position.

Start your slide steps to the racket side. Quickly make the pivot (turn). Get ready for the forehand stroke. Pivot back to the ready position, and start the slide steps toward the opposite direction. Pivot forward with the free-side foot and get ready for a backhand stroke. Pivot back and repeat the movements in the opposite direction again until you have completed them five times. Work on making all your motions smooth, relaxed, comfortable, and automatic. You should never have to stop and think how best to go after the ball. You will soon know that you are beginning to move like a tennis player.

LET'S ADD THE BALL!

Now that you have learned how to hold a racket and how to move your feet and body, it's time to introduce a few tips about the ball in tennis. You will learn much more about the ball by trying the drills at the end of this chapter and in later chapters.

Your first job as a tennis player is to try to see the ball hit the strings of your racket. The very center of the racket head is always the best spot. Every time the ball touches the strings of your racket, your eyes should see it touch. Don't just "feel" for the ball—watch it! Top players train themselves to see the ball meet the racket strings. So should you!

Here is one simple way to help you get an early start in training yourself. Get into your regular ready position. Have your knees bent with the racket out in front. Take a forehand grip, and turn the racket face down toward the ground (with your knuckles up) so it is about chest-high and level with the ground. Drop a ball from your free hand, and with your racket, quickly tap the ball downward ten times in a row. Keep the ball under control. Try tapping the ball onto the same spot on the court, using the center of your racket strings. Keep your eyes on the ball. Watch it hit the strings every time!

HELPFUL HINTS

1. Grip the racket firmly for good control but never grip it too tightly. If you keep too tight a grip all the time, you will tire your muscles. When you make contact with the ball, you can "squeeze" the grip for better control.
2. Keep the racket in a head-up position at all times. Don't let the wrist and the head of your racket sag or droop. Even when you are just carrying the racket, get in the habit of keeping your wrist up.

TAPPING BALL WITH HAND

TAPPING BALL DOWNWARD

TAPPING BALL UPWARD

43

3. Stay light on your feet at all times, ready to move. Never let your full body weight rest on flat feet unless the ball is not in play.

4. Remember to practice the ready position and sliding from one side to the other until you can do them without stopping to think.

5. Experienced players check the tennis-court surface. Is it clay, grass, cement, black-top, wood, or another type of artificial surface? This may help you decide whether it is best to use a sliding, stepping, skipping, or shuffling motion to move from one area of the court to another.

6. Don't spend time on any new racket grips. They are for the more experienced players. You can pick these up later after you have mastered the ground strokes and have grown stronger.

7. Watch the ball! Watch it closely enough so that you can begin to see the label or trademark on the ball. Many points are lost in a tennis match because the player does not watch the ball closely enough.

8. Remember to think, "I am a tennis player." Even when you practice. Knowing you are a tennis player will help you have good moves, confidence, and a lot more fun!

PRACTICE DRILLS

Find a safe place to practice. Look for indoor or outdoor practice areas at home. Hand-grip practice can be done anywhere. You can bounce a ball and do footwork movements on the driveway, sidewalk, or lawn. Try to locate nearby indoor gymnasiums and outdoor tennis courts in parks or school grounds.

Begin your drills with slow-action moves and work toward the faster-action drills as you improve.

GRIPPING DRILLS

1. With your free hand, hold the racket in an upright position with the *tip* on the ground. With your racket hand, shake hands with the handle of the racket. Check to see if you have the proper *forehand grip*. Repeat this action several times until it feels comfortable.

2. Take a forehand grip on the racket. Hold the throat portion with your free hand. Make a quarter-turn inward with the racket hand so you have completed a *backhand grip*. Release the grip and repeat this action until you can do it smoothly.

FOOTWORK DRILLS

Check the kind of turf or surface you plan to use. If a tennis court is not available, look for some other smooth surface area. Try this *sliding drill.*

1. Take your favorite forehand grip. Stand at the imaginary spot where the center line

meets the base line of a tennis court. Face the net in the correct ready position.

    a. Start your *slide* or *shuffle* across the base line to the far racket-side sideline. Begin your slides back to the starting point (center line).

    b. Begin your slide steps to the opposite sidelines.

    c. Return once again with smooth slide steps toward your racket side until you reach the center-line starting point.

Practice changing to the different grips while you are on the move. Practice keeping your body from bobbing up and down. Repeat this drill ten times. Speed up the action as you improve.

2. The "closed X" *sliding drill.* Get into a ready position at the center-line starting point as you did in the last drill. Practice changing your grip, body position, and footwork from start to finish while on the move.

    a. Begin by making your favorite footwork shuffles, slides, or steps toward the *far-right sideline corner.*

    b. Make a quarter-pivot (turn) so that the left shoulder points toward the *left corner of the net.* Start your smooth slides to that corner.

    c. Make a quarter-pivot (turn) so that your right shoulder points directly toward the sideline near the net. As you face the net, start your slide steps across the length of the net until you reach the *right corner of the net.*

d. Make a quarter-pivot (turn) back so that your left shoulder points toward the far left corner sideline. Start your sliding motion until you reach the *far-left sideline corner and base line.*

e. Make another quarter-pivot (turn) back so your shoulder points toward the opposite end of the base line and sideline. Slide to the center-line starting point to end the drill.

You have completed a "closed X" drill on your side of the court. Practice the same drill again, but this time begin your first slides to the left.

3. Make up your own footwork drills. If a tennis court is available, use its markings for your drills. If not, find a smooth surface, and make your own patterns with letters of the alphabet. The capital letters M, N, S, and U are challenging patterns. Figures zero, two, three, five, and eight are also fancy patterns to practice.

BOUNCING BALL DRILLS

You are going to practice *bouncing the ball down-ward.*

1. Get a tennis ball and bounce it onto the ground with the palm of your racket hand

just as you would dribble a basketball. Keep your knees bent, and practice keeping your eyes on the ball.

2. Pick up your racket and take a forehand grip. Get your body, knees, and racket in the ready position. Turn the racket face down toward the ground. Release the ball held in your free hand, and try to tap the ball twenty times in a row without losing control of it. Try tapping the ball on the same spot on the floor, and watch the ball hit the center of the strings. *Challenge a partner* to see who can keep the ball going more times without a miss.

3. Go through the same drill but tap the ball lower and faster by bending your knees slightly lower.

Try these drills *bouncing the ball upward.*

1. Take a forehand and ready position once more, but this time turn the racket face upward with your palm up. Start tapping the ball upward into the air just over your head. Watch the ball hit the center of the strings on every upward tap. Try to keep from having to chase the ball around the court. Can you stand in one spot for every tap? Can you go up to fifty controlled taps into the air? How many taps in a row can a partner or member of your family complete without moving?

2. Here is a drill that's a little tricky. It chal-

lenges your timing, accuracy, and eye-arm-hand grip abilities. *You start by tapping the ball softly into the air with one side of the racket strings and then the other.* Keep the forehand grip throughout the drill. Make the first tap at the ball with the palm up. Then, while the ball is still in the air, quickly and smoothly turn the racket hand so that your knuckles point up and tap the ball again into the air. Repeat this same action until you have made fifty controlled upward taps in a row. If you find the drill too difficult, try it with a two-handed grip. But always go back and see what you can do with one hand.

4

Forehand-Backhand: The Groundstroke Game

A schoolgirl tennis champion was trailing badly in a title match while her opponent kept the pressure on by scoring points. Suddenly she began to come back with thunderous forehand and backhand strokes that eventually helped her to win the match.

Another duel took place between two boy finalists to determine the school championship. Bobby kept his opponent, Eddie, scurrying from side to side with his clever backhand placement shots. Eddie was playing well, but often he was forced to lunge desperately while making backhand strokes, which were his greatest weakness. Bobby's groundstrokes never failed him throughout the match. He continued to make perfectly placed backhand and forehand strokes to force Eddie to hit backhanded approach shots into the net. Bobby eventually won the match.

These are only two of many examples that point out the importance of learning the groundstroke game.

HEART OF THE GAME

The groundstrokes are often known as the "heart" or "cornerstone" of the game of tennis. They are forehand and backhand strokes made by hitting the ball *after* it bounces once. The *forehand* is the groundstroke that is used to hit a ball that travels deep on your *racket side.* The *backhand* is the ground stroke that you will use for a ball that travels deep on the *opposite side* of your racket hand.

It is best for you to learn these strokes at the same time. After you finish working on one stroke, you should immediately spend the same amount of time practicing the other stroke. You must not learn one stroke well and forget the other. Too many beginning players spend almost all of their practice time on the forehand strokes. They neglect to learn all about the backhand strokes. This kind of practice is wrong. It will keep you from enjoying and playing your best game. It's like a soccer player who kicks well only with the right foot and poorly with the left. Or, a baseball player who fields a ball easily on one side and poorly on the other side.

For a better all-around game, develop both strokes by spending equal time on each. This practice will pay off when you step onto the court, because these strokes are used often, especially near the base line, for long, deep shots.

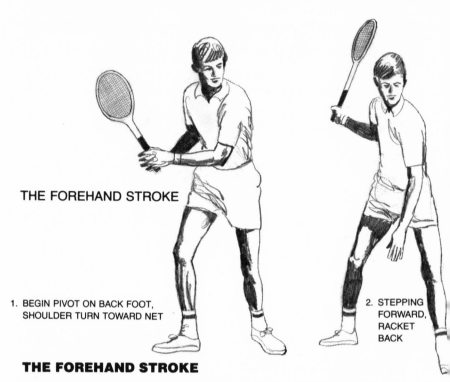

THE FOREHAND STROKE

1. BEGIN PIVOT ON BACK FOOT,
   SHOULDER TURN TOWARD NET

2. STEPPING
   FORWARD,
   RACKET
   BACK

THE FOREHAND STROKE

The whole idea in making the forehand stroke is to work for rhythm and timing in your action from start to finish. This total action can be broken down into four parts. They are:

1. The pivot and racket preparation
2. The step toward the ball
3. The swing that contacts the ball
4. The follow-through

The Pivot. Let's see how well you remember the pivot step. This time you will concentrate a little more on your *racket preparation.* Here it is again:

1. Take a ready position with a forehand grip

3. SWING WITH WEIGHT ON FRONT FOOT, EYES ON BALL

4. FOLLOW-THROUGH

and stand facing the net just behind an imaginary base line. Make two slide steps to the racket side. At the same time, bring your racket back. You are now ready to move into the forehand stroking position.

2. Start a smooth quarter-pivot turn toward your racket side. Make sure that you make the pivot motion with both feet at the same time.

3. The shoulder opposite your racket side should now be pointing toward the net. Your knees are bent and your eyes are on the ball.

4. Your weight continues to stay solidly and comfortably on the racket-side foot. The opposite foot is ready for a step toward the net.

The Step.

1. Your forehand racket grip is firm, and you begin your backswing motion to draw the arm and racket back. Get your racket back into position as soon as possible so that you will not be forced to rush your stroke at the ball.
2. Release the throat of the racket with your free hand, and hold that hand in front of you for body balance, while you draw the racket back.
3. With your weight solidly on the racket-side foot, lift your opposite foot a trifle, and make a shoulder-width step toward the on-coming ball. Start to shift your weight toward the forward (free) foot.
4. The shoulder and hip opposite the racket side shift a little forward toward the net in preparation for stroking the ball.
5. Keep your racket back in ready position about hip-high. Your arm should be almost fully stretched with only a small bend at the elbow.
6. You are ready for the swing at the ball.

Remember. Always get your *racket back* as quickly as possible for every stroke *before* making your stepping motion. Many players wait until the last moment to get the racket back. This often makes it too late for them to hit the ball correctly.

The Swing.

1. Your eyes keep watching the ball coming toward you.
2. Your racket grip is locked and firm, ready to make the racket swing.
3. The front hip and your racket-side foot are ready to twist and uncoil toward the net like a spring, as you begin to swing the racket head forward to meet the ball.
4. Shift your weight onto the inside portion of the front foot. Raise the heel of the opposite foot and point the toes toward the net.
5. Meet the ball just ahead of your forward foot at about waist height. With a flat racket face you stroke *through the ball*.
   Note: This is the point when your whole body and racket must act together to move toward the ball.

Follow-Through.

1. Continue to keep your eyes on the ball.
2. After contact with the ball, keep your racket on the ball as long as possible so that you don't cut down on your swing too soon. If you stop your swing early, your hit will travel long and out.
3. Stretch your body and racket arm toward the ball after the ball is completely stroked. This last action guarantees a smooth follow-through.

THE BACKHAND STROKE

1. START SHOULDER TURN,
PIVOT ON BACK FOOT

4. End up with your body facing the net and the ball of your racket foot still in contact with the ground. If you must keep from falling forward, quickly let the racket foot move forward and alongside the other foot.

At the end of each stroke, move swiftly back to the ready position to await your opponent's next shot. Now that you have an idea of the forehand stroke, let's find out how the backhand stroke is made.

THE BACKHAND STROKE

The *backhand stroke* is the groundstroke that is used to hit a ball that travels opposite your racket side. You start the stroke with the same ready

3. SWING WITH WEIGHT ON FORWARD FOOT, EYE ON BALL

2. STEPPING FORWARD, RACKET BACK, SHOULDER TOWARD NET

4. FOLLOW-THROUGH

stance used for the forehand shot. The total action is again broken down into four parts: the *pivot,* the *step,* the *swing,* and the *follow-through.*

Pretend that you are going after a ball on the backhand side. Here is what you do.

The Pivot.

1. Move quickly into a ready position with a backhand racket grip. Make two slide steps opposite your racket side. At the same time, bring your racket back.
2. Make a swift, smooth pivot toward your free side by turning on the ball of your racket-side foot and a little on the ball of the other foot.

3. Your weight is now a little more on the back foot. The racket head is held up, with your free hand controlling it behind you about hip-high.
4. Your racket-side shoulder and hip face the net, with the racket elbow a little lower than the other.
5. Your eyes follow the ball well before it bounces.

The Step.

1. *Push off* with the back foot and quickly make a shoulder-width step *toward the ball* with your racket-side foot. The toes should be pointing slightly toward the net at a 45-degree angle.
2. As your front hip moves forward, the weight shifts onto the inside portion of the racket foot.

The Swing.

1. Keep a solid grip on the racket. Quickly release the free hand from the racket and leave it at your side for balance.
2. With the racket arm almost straight you begin to lean forward as the swing begins. Start the swing by "uncoiling" your hips and face the net.
3. Turn on the ball of the back foot until that foot points toward the net. At the same

RIGHT HANDED—TWO HAND
BACKHAND STROKE

LEFT HANDED—TWO HAND
BACKHAND STROKE

time, your front shoulder is turning out as the stroke continues.

4. With the racket a little ahead of your wrist and elbow, make a swift, smooth *strike* at

the ball. You should meet the ball well ahead of your forward foot by about 4 to 5 inches. Did you see the ball hit the racket?

The Follow-Through.

1. Get your racket to follow the direction of the ball as long as possible.
2. Keep both feet on the ground throughout the action. If you must keep yourself from falling forward, rapidly bring the back foot forward alongside the racket foot.
3. Quickly get back to your favorite ready position on the court to return any ball hit over the net by your opponent.

Work for good *rhythm* and *timing* in your backhand stroke. Do this by following the same instructions that were given to you earlier for the forehand stroke.

RHYTHM AND TIMING IN YOUR STROKE

Next time you watch your favorite tennis players in action, notice how their whole bodies move when they are about to contact the ball. Notice how their bodies are always in a good ready position to help them make a smooth and accurate stroke at the ball. The players worked on these points when they were young. They were after ways to improve their *rhythm* and *timing* skills. This is similar to a soccer player getting ready for a pivot kick into a ball, or a dancer learning a new step.

A Rhythm and Timing Exercise. You can learn to improve your timing while practicing by *counting the beats* of your tennis stroke. Here is one way to do it:

1. Get in ready position for the forehand or backhand stroke.
2. Get set to begin counting to yourself for the moves you are about to make.
3. Start by moving the racket up and back and *pivot* on counts one and two.
4. Start your move to lean into the imaginary ball and *step* on count three.
5. *Swing* to contact the ball on four.
6. *Follow through* and regain your balance on five and six.

The total count of your movements and beats look like this:

Moves: pivot step swing follow-through
Beats: 1, 2 3 4 5, 6

Practice these steps in slow motion and count to yourself. Speed up your action by speeding up your counting beat. Check to see if your timing and rhythm are improving.

WATCH YOUR RACKET-FACE POSITION!

How you hold the racket face when it contacts the ball determines whether the ball will travel to the right, left, too low, too high, or barely over the net. Here is how the ball will travel when you hold the racket face in the different positions.

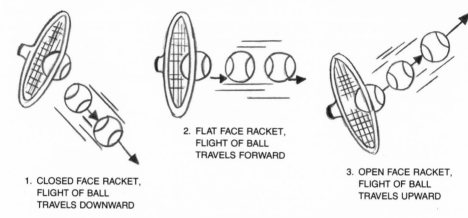

2. FLAT FACE RACKET, FLIGHT OF BALL TRAVELS FORWARD

1. CLOSED FACE RACKET, FLIGHT OF BALL TRAVELS DOWNWARD

3. OPEN FACE RACKET, FLIGHT OF BALL TRAVELS UPWARD

WATCH YOUR RACKET FACE POSITION!

1. If the racket face is parallel to the net when it contacts the ball, the ball should travel over the net.
2. If the racket face is tilted upward, the ball will go too high.
3. If the face is tilted downward, the ball will go too low.
4. In a forehand stroke, if the *tip* of the racket is pointed *away from the net* and the throat portion is closer to the net, the ball will travel toward the edge of the net or outside the sideline.
5. In a forehand stroke, if the *tip* of the racket is pointed *into the net* and the throat farther back from the net, the ball will travel toward the middle or opposite edge of the net.

STROKING THE BALL SOLIDLY!

To make a good solid hit, get into the habit of squeezing the handle just as you are about to meet the ball. Avoid holding the racket with a droopy or loose wrist. A loose wrist will cause your racket head to drop downward. Always be ready to make your groundstrokes with the racket head up as you are about to contact the ball. Don't overpower the swing or put all your muscle into it. But don't be too gentle either! For a good, solid stroke just *lean your body naturally* into the ball. *Leaning* will help the ball to travel with speed. You don't need an "all-out hard hit," which is hard to control and often causes mistakes.

KNOW HOW THE BALL WILL BOUNCE!

Did you know that scientists and teachers study the physical laws that tell how a ball bounces? Here are some simple rules you must understand about getting ready to strike a moving ball hit by your opponent.

1. A ball hit by your opponent will *bounce off* your side of the court at the same angle, arc, and speed that it took to *bounce onto* the court.
2. If your opponent's ball travels high over the net, it will also bounce high off the ground on your side of the court.
3. If the opponent's ball comes in low, it will also bounce low.

Knowing these rules will help you judge what the trajectory of the ball will be after it bounces. Keeping these rules in mind will give you time to get yourself and the racket in good position for the next stroke. Also remember:

1. Don't charge the ball.
2. Don't run up to the spot where it bounces. Let it come to you naturally.
3. As soon as the ball leaves your opponent's racket, *decide instantly* if you plan to use a forehand or backhand stroke and start bringing your racket back.
4. Don't wait until the ball bounces to take your racket back. This is too late and it will cause you to rush your swing.

HELPFUL HINTS

1. As soon as your opponent hits the ball, decide instantly what you believe the height and speed of the bounce will be.
2. Don't lead with the elbow on the backhand when you are about to stroke the ball. Get your racket head to the ball first.
3. Don't stop as you strike the ball. Let your racket follow through on the ball as long as you can.
4. Don't move too close to the ball as you swing. Keep in mind that your racket is fairly long. There should be enough distance between you and the ball to allow you to extend your arm and your racket.

5. For a firm grip and stroke, squeeze your racket just as you make contact with the ball.
6. Get into the habit of looking at the ball as it touches your racket strings.
7. As soon as you finish your follow-through, get yourself back to center and the racket back into a ready position for a return swing.

DRILLS

Most of the following drills can be done alone and with or without equipment. Some require a partner. You may also try to locate a safe indoor gym or outdoor area that has a fence or solid wall to stop a ball that is hit over a real or imaginary net.

1. Open your racket hand and go through the motions of a forehand and backhand stroke without a racket. Look into a mirror to check yourself. Make the same movements with a racket in your hand.
2. Take a forehand or backhand grip and start bouncing the ball to the floor with the racket, as you would dribble a basketball. Start a racket dribble bounce while you are walking. On a slow run. Challenge a partner to a race. See how many racket dribbles you can make without a miss.
3. Put a marker on a wall about 36 to 42 inches from the floor. Stand a good distance back, drop a ball a little in front and to the side of

you, and practice your forehand and backhand strokes. Can you hit the ball just above the marker? Can you see the ball meeting your racket?

4. Have a partner drop one ball at a time straight down a little in front and to either your forehand or backhand side. Using your smoothest stroke, try to get the ball to travel just about a foot or two over the net. If a net is not available, aim for a marker on the wall.

5. Get your partner to stand about one foot away from your forehand side. Have the partner stretch one arm in front of you with the hand open and fingers spread on the face of your racket. Start a *slow motion* forehand stroke while your partner presses against the strings. As you continue to press against the hand, move through the entire forehand swing. Did you feel the *pressure* against your racket? This is the feeling you get when you lean and stroke into the ball. Try this from the backhand side.

6. Try the same drill once again. As you complete your swing, have your partner suddenly slide his or her hand toward the tip of the racket, and then grab it, and pull it and you forward. To catch your balance, you quickly let your racket-side foot drag forward. This is the action that gives you a smooth follow-through.

7. Have a partner stand on the opposite side of the court:

FEEL THE PRESSURE AGAINST YOUR RACKET!

    a. Have your partner toss balls over the net for you to practice the backhand and forehand strokes. Try the strokes after the ball takes one bounce.

    b. Start a rally with both of you holding a racket. Don't try to win points. Try aiming the ball directly at each other so you will have more practice hits. See how long you can keep the rally going using only the forehand and backhand groundstrokes. Remember always to turn your side to the net.

Not everyone can find a safe space or a real court for practice sessions. *Practice Equipment for Everyone* in Chapter Ten and *More Help Getting Started* in Chapter Eleven will give you additional ideas on how you can practice safely using the least amount of space and equipment.

5

The Big Serve

Most people like to test their accuracy in hitting the "bull's-eye." The tennis serve offers you the chance to see just how accurately you can place the ball inside your opponent's service court. The service stroke is the only stroke that each player can control fully. That's because no interference is allowed to prevent you from making a good shot.

The serve is a beautiful stroke. Fans like to see a player smash the ball hard into the opposite service court. It will take practice and patience, so don't get discouraged if things don't go well at first. With practice you will soon discover the joy in making the big serve.

THE STROKE THAT STARTS THE GAME

The *service* or *serve* is the action that starts the

game in tennis. You learned earlier that you have two chances to serve the ball within your opponent's service court. Failure to do this means that you have committed a double fault and that you will lose a point to your opponent.

A "POINT-GETTER" STROKE

The serve is often known as a quick point-getter play. That's because you can win a point without giving your opponent an opportunity to hit the ball back to you. To do this you must have *control, accuracy,* and *speed* with your service hit. It's a good idea for beginning players to work for control and accuracy first. You can work on speed later as you improve.

DIFFERENT SERVICE STROKES

There are several kinds of service strokes. Players have their favorites. The *slice, flat serve,* and *twist* are some names given to them.

The *twist* is difficult to make. It's called the twist because the player tosses the ball upward a little behind the head and toward the free shoulder side, and has to bend his or her back in order to hit the ball. The ball is hit with a twisting inside-and-out racket motion that is difficult to control.

In a *flat serve* the ball has almost no spin. The ball is usually tossed above and in front of the racket shoulder, then hit in a straight line from the racket face to the opponent's service court. Too often beginners use the flat serve because they are

2. SLICE SERVE

1. FLAT SERVE

3. TWIST SERVE

**DIFFERENT BALL TOSSES AND BODY
POSITIONS ON SERVE**

anxious just to get the ball into the target area. This fear can get you into the habit of making a poor serve that travels slowly and arcs into the opponent's court like a "blooper." Serves of this kind are easy for your opponent to return and thus score points.

The *slice* serve is the one most popularly used by both the beginning and top players. It is sometimes called the "spin" serve. This is the serve that will be described to you below. *Put your time and practice on the slice serve.* It may seem a little difficult for you at first, but stay with it. By the time you go through the hints and drills, you will begin to feel confidence in making your own big serve.

SERVICE STROKE ACTION

The tennis serve is made with one, continuous, non-stop action. But to have a better understanding of the full action, it is broken down for you into six parts. Every part is important.

1. Stance position
2. Racket grip
3. Ball toss
4. Swing
5. Hit
6. Follow-through

Pretend you are ready to make the first serve of the game from the right side of the court. Go through all the movements in slow motion without using a ball. Here is the way each part of the action is made.

The Stance. Take your ready service position a little to the right of the center mark, behind the base line. Have a racket in one hand and a make-believe ball in the other.

1. Face the sideline but turn the free side of your body just a trifle toward the net.
2. Position the free side of your body (the side with the imaginary ball in the hand) toward the net. The racket side is away from the net and positioned toward the fence behind you.
3. Point your front (free) side foot forward but turn it a little inward toward your body.
4. Place your racket side (rear) foot about one-half step closer than the front foot to the side line you are facing. There are also about 10 to 18 inches between your feet. Your rear foot is parallel to the base line.
5. You are in a ready stance position with weight equally distributed on both feet.

The Grip.

1. Take a grip on the racket that is halfway between a forehand and a backhand grip. One way to do this is to take a regular forehand grip and then make one-eighth of a turn inward with the same hand. This is known as a *service* or *continental* grip on the racket.
2. Keep your "trigger" (first) finger slightly apart from the other fingers.
3. The "V" shape formed between the thumb and first finger is seen on top and a little toward the inside of the racket. Be careful not to make the mistake of gripping the

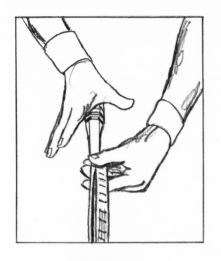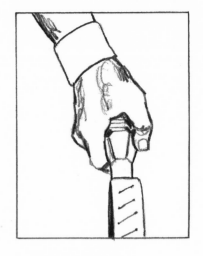

1. START OF GRIP

2. COMPLETE GRIP

THE SERVICE (CONTINENTAL) GRIP

racket with the entire palm flat over the handle.

4. Hold your wrist more loosely than you do in the other strokes. To keep a firm hold on the racket, squeeze the handle at the moment you hit the ball.

5. Hold the racket about waist-high. Its head is pointed slightly upward and toward the opponent's service court. The throat of the racket is resting lightly on the fingers of your ball hand.

The Ball Toss. Make believe you have a ball in your free hand. Go through all the action as if you were going to toss a real ball for the serve. You must work to coordinate the timing of the toss with the movement of the racket swing. (The swing is explained after the toss.)

1. Rest the imaginary ball on your fingertips —not on the palm of your hand.
2. Start to shift your weight onto the back (racket-side) foot as you are about to start your toss.
3. Begin to lean a little to the rear until you form a small arch in your back. The rear (racket) leg remains almost straight. The front knee is bent and the heel of the foot is raised.
4. Lift the arm with the ball gently upward until it is fully straight. At the height of your

SERVER-RECEIVER COURT POSITION

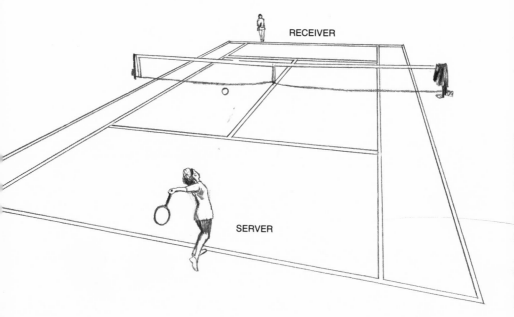

RECEIVER

SERVER

1. READY STANCE FOR TOSS   2. THE TOSS

reach, toss, shove, or push the ball upward off the first or the first two fingertips and thumb. The fingers and palm both face the sky at the end of the toss. Your toss should rise to about one-half of a racket length higher than the point where you will contact the ball.

5. The ball should rise in the air high enough so that you can hit it with the center of the

3. FULL BACKSWING

4. THE HIT, EYE ON BALL,
   READY FOR FOLLOW-THROUGH

racket strings when your arm and racket are completely straight. The ball will be about 6 inches away from your racket side and 12 inches in front of your body.

6. You are ready to make a service stroke that will give you a slice on the ball.

NOTE: While you were moving to make the toss, your racket arm and racket were also in motion. *The action of both arms actually begins at the same time.* Here is the racket-arm action that goes on while you are making your toss.

The Racket Swing. The swing for the service is sometimes known as the wind-up for the service. The swing can be a *full* (complete) swinging motion or a *short* (modified) swinging motion. Many beginning players learn the short swing first and the full swing after they improve. Both swings are explained for you. Here is how to make the short swing.

The Short (Modified) Swing. Start by placing the racket arm over your service-side shoulder. You eliminated the beginning of the full wind-up.

1. You should practically feel the racket "scratching" against your back. The racket hand is over the racket shoulder with the racket pointing down along your back.
2. The imaginary ball is tossed into the air for the serve.
3. The racket elbow is held high with the forearm level (parallel) with the ground.
4. Start to uncoil (turn) your racket shoulder and hip toward the net. Keep your eye on the ball.
5. Begin to shift your weight from the rear foot to the ball of the front foot. At the same time *start your arm motion upward with the wrist starting the action first.* (Think of the wrist action as if you were hammering a nail above your head and into the air.)

READY FOR SHORT (MODIFIED)
SERVICE SWING

6. Continue to move the whole racket arm and shoulder straight up. The racket should almost brush the hair on the back of your neck. Your arm straightens up with your racket and shoulder stretching as high as you can reach.

The action should feel as if you had tossed or swung the racket as high as possible. Now you are ready for the hit.

The Hit.

1. Your eyes are on the ball.

2. The racket strings face the net, ready for contact with the ball.
3. Keep your wrist just a little ahead of the racket—ready for the wrist snap.
4. You're on the balls of both feet with the weight shifting well onto the front foot. *Your whole racket side continues to uncoil, turn, and lean toward the ball and net.*
5. With a good "snap" of the wrist, *hit* into and over the ball, which should be well out in front and above the side of your racket shoulder. This will give the ball an "over-spin" or "slice" action.

The Follow-Through.

1. Keep reaching with your racket toward the ball and in the direction of your opponent's service area.
2. Relax your racket arm by letting it drop across the other side of our body. Don't try to stop the forward-downward motion of the racket.
3. As your body continues to lean forward, get your racket-side foot to drag or slide forward to stop yourself from falling.
4. Quickly get back into a ready position to go after a ball that may be returned by your opponent.

That's all there is to it! With practice you may discover that it's almost like throwing a ball for distance.

The Full Swing. Here are the additional instructions for practicing the *full swing.* Get into a ready position.

1. The racket throat rests lightly over the fingers of the ball hand. You are ready as you were earlier to make an imaginary toss, but now you will also begin the racket swing at the same time.
2. Keep your racket arm relaxed. Begin to shift your weight onto the racket-side foot.
3. As you're about to toss the ball, let the racket swing start downward and back until the racket is pointing toward the fence or backstop behind you. The racket arm, elbow, and racket are straight.
4. Your front knee is bent and your front hip and shoulder are pointing toward the net.
5. Make a smooth and steady motion by bringing your racket elbow, forearm, and racket into the same back-scratching position that you took for the start of your short swing. *Do not stop the action here.* Complete the swing in one solid, continuous motion to hit the ball as you did earlier.

Try all the same service actions with a tennis ball.

FIRST SERVE VS. SECOND SERVE

Next time you watch your favorite player, notice if the first serve is a stronger hit than the second. Most players try to "blast" their first serve as hard as they can. If such a ball lands in the opponent's service court, it is very difficult for the receiver to return the ball safely. But many players, especially beginners, miss the target and take a service fault. The server then must make the next serve good or a point goes to the opponent. This situation often results in the server trying too carefully to make the second serve good. That's why the second serve of many players is often a little "pitty-pat" kind of stroke that bloops into the opponent's court. The ball in this case is not too difficult for the opponent to put away. A strong hit for a good point return!

Server's Choice of Hit. Players must make an early choice on how they wish to play the first and second serves. Most top players make their first and second serves look almost the same. Here is what they do! They make the first serve harder for the receiver by putting more power, lean, and follow-through into the stroke. If the first serve is not good, they make the second serve with the same motion and almost the same power. The only difference in the second serve is a little less lean and more topspin over the ball. This gives the server less ball speed, but better control.

A big first serve with lots of power and lean gives the server a better chance to get close to the net faster. The second serve usually has less speed, so the server is more likely to take a position closer to the base line after the hit.

Try your practice serves with the same motion. If you don't make the first serve good, just lessen up a bit on your power and speed. Work for control and accuracy.

HELPFUL HINTS

1. Before you start the service motion, position the free side of your body toward the net.
2. Relax your full arm and shoulder during the whole service motion. Keep the palm of your racket hand facing the net throughout the serving action.
3. You may squeeze the handle for a firm grip on the racket as contact with the ball is made. But try to keep your wrist loose.
4. Always use the service grip when serving.
5. Let the ball "slip-slide" off your fingertips. Don't throw it into the air.
6. If your toss is too high, you are in danger of hitting the ball high in the air.
7. If your toss is too low, you will be unable to extend your arm fully. The ball will most likely go into the net, and you will lose power.
8. If your toss is too close to your body, your cramped position will cause you to lose a smooth swing.
9. If the toss is too far in front, you are apt to hit the ball into or below the net.
10. If the toss is over and behind your head, you will tend to hit the ball too long and too high.

11. After completing your serve, always get back into a ready position to hit an opponent's return ball.

There are many ways you can practice to improve your tennis serve. You can practice indoors or outdoors, alone or with a partner.

A real tennis court is fine if you can find one. If one is not available, look for a smooth wall and draw a line on it at the height of a net. Draw another marker on the ground, showing the distance of the base line from the net. Another idea is to fasten an old carpet or piece of canvas or net between two trees. Many tennis courts have a backboard at one end of the fence for players to use for practice. Look for the best places to practice.

1. *Without a racket or ball.* Go through the whole action of making the service stroke.
2. Practice making the ball toss only. Are your eyes on the ball? Is the ball at the right spot? Go through the full swinging motion, but do not hit the ball.
3. *With a ball in place of the racket.* Have a tennis ball in the racket hand. Take the regular service-ready position. Go through the *service action* and see if you can toss it into the opponent's service area. Challenge a partner to see who can put the ball into the target area most often.
4. Get ready with a ball and racket. Make a

base-line marker 39 feet from a wall, back-board, or carpet. Draw a line on the back-board showing the same height of the net. Using the *short swing* (modified) serve, see how many balls you can hit just over the line. Practice the *full swing* once you gain confidence with the short swing.

5. *Practice on a real court.* Have as many tennis balls as possible on hand. Using the short swing, see how many times out of ten tries you can serve the ball into your opponent's right service court. Collect the tennis balls and make ten more serves. How many were you able to put into your opponent's right service court? Challenge a partner to a service contest!

6. Try the same drill as above, but put the serve into your opponent's left service court.

7. After you have gained confidence with the short swing, do the same drills using the full swing.

8. If you are really getting good, try aiming your serve at a specific spot in the service area.

9. *Partner drill on a real court.* Have a partner act as your opponent ready to return your serve. See how many service shots out of ten you can keep your opponent from returning safely. Change positions and see how many serves your opponent can keep you from returning.

6

Make Those Volleys Count

Players, coaches, and fans constantly read and hear about a stroke players make from near the net area. This special stroke is usually made by players who have already learned to use the earlier ground-strokes very well. The name of the stroke is the *volley*.

As you continue to play the game you will find that there are times when you need this additional skill to keep up with more experienced players. You will also discover that the volley stroke gives you another way to score points.

THE VOLLEY

The *volley stroke* can be an important part of your tennis game. To volley means *to hit an opponent's ball in the air before it bounces*. The stroke is usually made when you are near the net area. You will see it more in the doubles game than in the singles game. Players and sports writers call this action the "net game."

When to Use the Volley. When you are close to the net, the volley stroke can be used as an *offensive shot* to score points. It is used as a defensive stroke when you are forced to hit your opponent's ball on the fly. If you don't hit it on the fly, the ball will travel past you and score a point for your opponent. This means you cannot let the ball bounce to give you more time to get into position to use your favorite groundstroke.

Volley Grip. There are three popular grips that players use to make the volley stroke.

1. Forehand grip
2. Backhand grip
3. Service or Continental grip

The *forehand* and *backhand grips* are the same grips you used for the forehand and backhand shots. The *service* or *Continental* grip is the same one you used to make the serve.

Beginning players often have a difficult time deciding which grip to use when they go for a volley stroke. That's because players are never sure to what side of the body the opponent will force them to make the shot. There may be times when they are forced to use a forehand grip to make a backhand volley shot. Or they are caught with a backhand grip and must make a forehand or overhead shot.

If your opponent seems to be giving you time to shift into your best grip for volley shots, keep using this style of play. But if you are getting caught making your volley strokes with a weak grip, you should practice being in a ready position with a service grip. The service grip is taken halfway between the position of the forehand and backhand grips. This grip gets you in better ready position for almost any kind of volley strokes.

Approaching the Net for the Volley. Let's get ready to make a volley shot. Which grip will you use? Will you have time to rush close to the net to make the stroke? Here is what you do.

Pretend that during a rally (game) you are standing between your base line and the service line. A ball comes toward you. You hit it well back near your opponent's base line. You are thinking ahead! It's time to try a volley stroke on your next return shot. *You decide to get in ready position with a service grip on the racket.*

1. Rush toward the net and *come to a quick stop* between your service line and the net. You're now in position to go after any kind of volley shot.
2. Hold the racket in front and away from your chest with the free hand on the throat for added control. Look!
3. Your opponent is returning the ball over to your forehand side at about the height of your head.

2. STEPS FORWARD, PUNCHING BALL WITH FIRM WRIST

1. APPROACHES NET, COMES TO QUICK STOP

3. KNEES LOW WITH RACKET UP ON FOLLOW-THROUGH

FOREHAND VOLLEY—USING CONTINENTAL GRIP

Making the Volley Stroke. You are facing the net with bent knees and your weight evenly distributed on the soles of your feet. Your eyes are glued on the ball.

1. You turn quickly toward the ball by taking a sharp step forward and inward with the foot of your free side. *The free side shoulder is pointed toward the net.*
2. The racket head is held ready slightly higher than your hand. The racket face is in "closed" or slightly downward position.
3. Tighten your racket grip. With hardly any backswing, you are about to meet the ball

on the fly when it arrives just in front of you.
4. With good elbow and lower arm action, make a "punch" or "jab" swing at the ball, using very little follow-through motion.

This completes the action for a good, head-high forehand volley stroke made with a service racket grip. Each player must decide whether to gamble by waiting until the last moment to shift into the different grips before making the shot. The more you practice the volley stroke, the earlier you will discover which grip works best for you. For now, start by using the service grip. The whole idea is to work on your *timing* of the total body action from start to finish. For example:

1. Rush toward the net for a good volley position.
2. Decide early on the best racket grip to use.
3. Move into the ball by turning your body until your shoulder is pointing toward the net.
4. Meet the ball with a solid punch, using very little backswing or follow-through.

More Volley Shots. The *backhand volley shot* is made in the same way as the forehand volley stroke. The big difference is that you will move into the ball with your racket foot and the racket side of your body. You have a choice whether to try the stroke with a backhand grip or stay with a service grip.

To make a *low volley shot* you must bend way

LOW FOREHAND VOLLEY
—SHORT BACKSWING,
KNEES LOW, OPEN RACKET

down, almost touching the court with your knees if necessary. With your seat down and head up, you meet the ball with a good upward punch. This means that your *racket face must be open* (facing slightly upward). This helps to put enough "lift" or "loft" on the ball to carry it over the net. You will use the service grip unless you feel more comfortable with one of the others. The best grip to use for a low volley will often depend upon the side of your body to which the ball is hit.

A volley shot made for a ball coming straight toward you high over the net takes special care. You must be careful not to return the ball over your opponent's end line. This is a mistake that beginning players often make. The reason is that they

HIGH VOLLEY
WITH FOREHAND GRIP

HIGH VOLLEY
WITH BACKHAND GRIP

keep the racket strings facing straight forward. When you are forced to make a *high volley shot,* raise your racket head-high with the strings facing slightly downward. Meet the ball well in front of you and direct it over the net and down onto your opponent's court. Many players shorten up their grip for a high volley to keep the return volley from going over their opponent's base line.

Making a volley stroke for a ball that is hit directly to you demands perfect timing and quick action. That's because you will not have time to step aside and get set into your best striking and grip position. You have little choice but to meet the ball while it is coming straight at you. This means that you will have to *keep a tight grip and stiff wrist* with your favorite racket hand and grip. If necessary, you may use the free hand for a two-handed grip and support. Meet the ball in front of you with a nice jab or punch shot to put the ball over the net. How you hold the racket face will depend upon the height at which you were forced to meet the ball.

HELPFUL VOLLEY HINTS

1. Sometimes when the ball is being hit rapidly back and forth close to the net, you will not have time to keep changing from a forehand to a backhand grip and back again.
2. Start out by using the service or Continental grip for your volley shots.
3. As you continue to play, find out which grip works best for you for the different volley strokes.
4. Always try to turn your free side toward the net when you are ready to make the volley stroke.
5. If you don't have time to turn your feet around, make sure you at least get the free shoulder pointing toward the net when you meet the ball.
6. The distance you must step for your forehand and backhand volley shots will depend upon how far the ball is from the racket.
7. For a low volley shot, your racket strings must face a little upward (open-face position) to get the ball over the net.
8. For a high volley shot, your racket strings must face downward (closed-face position)

to get the ball within the opposite court area.

9. For a shoulder- or chest-high volley shot, your racket strings must face almost straight forward (flat-face position) toward the net.

10. Just try getting the ball safely onto your opponent's court when you first use the volley shots. As you gain experience, try *placing or hitting* the last ball before your volley shot well back toward the opponent's end line. An aggressive advance play (approach shot) gives you extra time to rush near the net so you can get into your favorite volley stroke position.

VOLLEY SHOT DRILLS

1. With your bare hand, hit a ball against a smooth wall over and over without letting the ball drop to the ground.

2. Have a partner stand a few feet in front of a fence or wall. You take a ready sideways position about 5 yards away with a racket. Ask your partner to make soft, underhand tosses to you on the fly about shoulder height, toward your forehand side. Backhand side. Directly to you. Over your head. Try just blocking the tossed ball so that it rebounds off your racket and back toward the wall.

3. Try the same drill. Instead of just blocking

the ball, put a little more punching action into your volley stroke.

4. Try these same volley shots with a ball being tossed directly in front of you about knee-high.

5. Get on a real court and have a partner stand about 3 yards behind the net. You take a position between the service line and the net on your side of the court. Have your partner make soft, underhand tosses on the fly so you can try the many different volley shots. When you start feeling confident, try placing or aiming your volleys at specific spots on the court. Check to see if you can see the ball meet your racket.

6. Have a partner stand near the base line with a racket. You take a position on the opposite court near the net area. Ask your partner to try striking the ball directly to you. To your right side. Left side. See how well you can return the ball onto your opponent's court with good action volley strokes.

7. Get your partner to take a position between the service line and the net. You take the same position on the other side of the net. Using only your bare hand, see how long you can volley the ball back and forth over the net. Practice this same drill with a racket. Notice how little time you have if you try to change grips for the different volley strokes.

7

What About Advanced Strokes?

What about those advanced strokes? When are they used? Should young boys and girls try them?

DON'T LOSE YOUR OTHER STROKES!

Before you go into the advanced strokes, make sure that you hold onto the ones you have already learned. Don't neglect them. Continue to use and improve them. As you grow older and begin to play with more experienced players, you will discover that additional skills are needed for you to keep up with your opponents' play. Here are some of the popular advanced strokes that will help you play a more well-rounded game.

1. The lob
2. The overhead smash
3. The half-volley

4. The drop shot
5. Topspin shots
6. Backspin shots

The *lob* is a stroke that is used to return the ball to your opponent with a high arc or curve. It is used mostly as a *defensive play.* You may use it as an *offensive shot* after you begin to feel comfortable with it. The racket grip and stroke are the same as in the forehand and backhand shots. In making the lob shot, you must hold your racket in a way that will get the ball well over your opponent's head and reach. You must keep from hitting the ball too short or too close to the net. This kind of lob gives your opponent too good a shot to score a point.

Making the Lob. Pretend that you are forced to run for a ball hit toward the sideline of your forehand side. You're too late for a good shot and you're way out of position. All you want to do is to prevent your opponent from scoring by not letting the ball go past you and give yourself time to get back to the center of the base line for the next shot. This is done by returning the ball with a *defensive lob stroke.* Here is what you do:

1. Go after the ball with a ready forehand grip.
2. Get your racket in position to meet the ball by using very little backswing or body and shoulder turn.
3. *Meet the ball* with the racket face open, or

tilted upward. Give it a good "jab," "push," or "lift" hit into the air well over your opponent's head if the opponent is standing near the net.

4. Make an upward follow-through, guiding the ball in its upward trajectory, and in the direction you want the ball to go; quickly get back into a more favorable court position, ready to return your opponent's next shot.

If your opponent forced you to chase a ball on the opposite court sideline, you would make a *backhand lob stroke.*

Lob Stroke Strategy. The lob requires that you

FOREHAND LOB—RACKET FACE OPEN WITH UPWARD SWING

make quick, on-the-spot decisions during the action play. You must be ready to ask yourself: Should I go for a defensive or offensive lob?

You should use the *defensive lob* when you know that you don't have time to get into position for one of your favorite strokes. When this happens all you do is try to lob the ball high over your opponent's head and well back near the base line. This kind of play gives you time to get back into your favorite court position, ready to handle any shot from your opponent.

The *offensive lob* shot should be used when your opponent is standing close to the net. You should try to lob the ball just out of your opponent's reach and near the base line for a possible point.

THE OVERHEAD SMASH

The overhead smash is one of the most exciting and dramatic strokes in tennis. It is often compared to the home run in baseball. The *overhead smash* is made with a powerful overhead swing that forces the ball to come down swiftly into the opponent's court. Players and fans also call the shot a "kill" because it usually scores a point for the hitter.

The grip, stance, body shift, swing, and follow-through are almost the same as those used in the serve. One big difference is that you do not need a full backswing as in the serve. Another important difference is that on the serve you have the ball in your hand for the toss, while on the overhead smash you are forced to move to the spot where your opponent hits the ball.

1. GETS UNDER BALL, RACKET STARTS BACK

2. REACHES HIGH FOR HIT WITH WEIGHT ON FRONT FOOT AND FOLLOW-THROUGH

THE OVERHEAD SMASH

Making the Overhead Smash. Pretend you are getting ready to *hit a ball on the fly* for an overhead smash. Make believe your opponent has hit you a high lob that is about to land between the net and your service line. Here is what you do to make an overhead smash.

1. Quickly size up or study the lob. Make a decision. Where will the ball land?
2. Take a service grip on the racket and, at the same time, start using short, sharp steps to run to the spot where you think the ball will land. Get yourself into a service stance with your free side closer to the net.
3. Your racket is poised in the air in a position just behind your head. Do not make a full service backswing. Use your short service swing instead.
4. Your free hand is pointing toward the ball for extra balance and accuracy. Start your striking motion by straightening your racket arm upward and forward.
5. Meet the fly ball with a good smash just as it reaches a level about arm and racket length above and in front of your head.
6. Follow through by shifting your weight from the back to the front foot just as you would for the service swing.

There are times when you may wish to make a smash shot after the ball takes a first high bounce. You will make the shot in the same way you did for a ball hit on the fly.

Smash-Shot Strategy. The best time to use a smash shot is when your opponent hits a weak lob between your service line and the net. You will have the choice to position yourself under the ball for a hit either on the fly or after the first high bounce. There will be times when it is best to let the ball bounce to give you more time to get set for a better smash and a sure point. This kind of play will take quick thinking and speed if you are to place the ball away from your opponent for a score. Another good idea is not to try smash shots from a position near your base line. This takes a lot of accuracy, and it also gives your opponent an advantage in returning the ball for a point.

HALF-VOLLEY STROKE

The half-volley is a fancy-looking shot. It is a stroke made when you hit the ball immediately after it touches the ground. You learned earlier that a regular volley stroke is made by hitting the ball on

1. BALL HITS GROUND, RACKET LOW

2. HITS BALL SOON AFTER BOUNCE

THE HALF-VOLLEY STROKE

the fly. The half-volley reminds many players and fans of the drop kick in football and soccer.

Most half-volley shots are made when a ball is hit near your feet, or barely within your racket reach. *The shot is taken when you have no choice but to stroke the ball immediately after it touches the ground.* For this reason it is usually considered a defensive stroke.

The grip, stance, and motion are practically the same as those used for the regular volley shot. There is very little backswing or follow-through. All you do is try to get the racket face to *block the ball* with a little punch or push motion immediately after it lands. How much you tilt the racket face will depend upon your position on the court. It may also depend upon where you wish to aim the ball onto your opponent's court. Be careful not to get too fancy. Train yourself just to get the ball onto your opponent's court.

THE DROP SHOT

The drop shot is one of the most delicate strokes in tennis. It is not often used, even by players who know the game well. A drop shot is made when the ball is hit or "chopped" so delicately and is given so much backspin that it barely clears the net and drops instantly with very little bounce. The shot usually scores a point if your opponent is standing well back and deep within the backcourt. If it does not score a point, it will at least force your opponent to make a long run for the ball and possibly make a poor shot.

1. STEPPING FORWARD,
   RACKET BEGINS DOWNWARD
   SWING TO MEET BALL

2. OPEN FACE RACKET CONTINUES
   DOWN AND FORWARD WITH
   SHORT FOLLOW-THROUGH

THE DROP SHOT

The grip, stance, and action for the drop shot are similar to your regular forehand and backhand groundstrokes. You make the drop shot work by going through all the *beginning moves* of a regular groundstroke. This should fool your opponent, who will think you are about to make the action of a full stroke. But then you slow up your swing just as you are about to contact the ball. Instead of a full swing, you hit the ball with a soft push or chop, using a short racket follow-through. A good drop shot will see the ball barely clear the net.

GETTING SPIN ON THE BALL

Skillful players often put extra spin on the ball. It helps to keep their opponents off guard. They are experts in making one or both of the following shots. Here are the most popular:

A Topspin or Overspin. This means that the ball spins forward after the hit. A ball hit with topspin usually bounces high just after contacting the ground. The topspin shot is most often made from your forehand groundstroke position. You hit with topspin by starting your swing with the racket head a little below the ball. You hit up, through, and over the ball. This forces it to spin forward or away from you. First start with a flat racket face and suddenly, on contacting the ball, tilt the racket forward or in a slightly closed position. With a good forward and upward follow-through swing, the racket head ends up a little higher than where the ball was contacted.

A Backspin or Underspin. This means that the ball spins backward after it is hit. It usually bounces low after contacting the ground. To hit with a backspin you should start your swing with the racket head a little above the height of the ball. Then you hit down, behind, and through the ball. This will force the ball to spin backward or toward you. The action looks like a chopping motion. The ball is contacted with the racket head tilted backward or in a slightly open position. You end the swing with a short follow-through. The shot is often taken from your backhand groundstroke position. You also learned earlier that backspin on the ball is used when you make a drop shot.

HINTS FOR ADVANCED STROKES

Hints for Lob.

1. A lob hit either too low or too short will give your opponent a good chance to return the ball for a score with an overhead smash.
2. The swing for the lob starts with very little backswing.
3. After lobbing the ball, get yourself back into a ready position for a possible return of your opponent's next shot.
4. Be ready at all times to make a quick decision whether to use the lob as a defensive or offensive shot.

Hints for Overhead Smash.

1. Make up your mind quickly! Are you going for a smash on a fly ball? Or after the first high bounce?
2. Use your best speed to get under the ball.
3. Try contacting the ball when it is well in front of you.
4. The best overhead smash shots are made from an area between your service line and the net.
5. Don't try smash shots from a position near your base line.

Hints for Half-Volley.

1. Get into the habit of using your racket to block the ball soon after it touches the ground.
2. Give the ball a follow-through "punch" or "shove" soon after contact.

Hints for Drop Shot.

1. Use the drop shot when your opponent is deep in the backcourt.
2. Meet the ball with a soft, downward, chopping motion.
3. Use very little backswing or follow-through.

Hints for Putting Spin on Ball.

1. Add *topspin* to your strokes by starting your backswing with the racket a little below the ball.
2. Add *backspin* by starting your backswing with the racket a little above the ball.

DRILLS FOR ADVANCED STROKES

Drills for Lob.

1. Have a partner stand a few feet from the net. You take a position near the base line on the opposite side of the net.
    a. Try tossing tennis balls over your partner's head so that the ball lands just inside the base line.

b. Make the same tosses while your partner holds his or her racket straight up over the head.
2. You and your partner take the same position as above. You are ready with a racket in your hand.
    a. Get your partner to make soft tosses to you.
    b. Hit the tosses with nice lobs that travel over your partner's head so that the ball lands safely in the backcourt.

Drills for Smash.

1. Have a partner stand about 3 to 5 feet from a fence or wall. You take a position about 7 to 10 yards away.
    a. Get your partner to make some easy lob tosses that travel high enough to force you to move under the ball.
    b. Try to direct overhead smash shots so they hit the wall behind your partner about 5 feet up from the ground.
    c. After every toss, have your partner spring to one side so he or she won't be hit by your smash.
2. Your partner takes a position near the base line of a court while you stand inside but near your service line.
    a. Your partner tosses you high, easy lobs between the net and your service line.

b. Sprint under the ball and practice your smash strokes.

c. As you begin to improve, ask your partner to mix up the tosses so that you are forced to move to your left, right, forward, or backward to get under the ball.

Drills for Half-Volley

1. Stand several yards away from a fence or wall. Have a ball in one hand and a racket in the other. With your arm stretched out and pointing toward the fence, drop the ball lightly in front of you. Step up and make a nice half-volley stroke soon after the ball touches the ground.

2. Have a partner stand near a wall, fence, or practice net. You take a position about 7 to 10 yards away.

   a. Get your partner to make easy tosses so that the ball lands about 3 feet in front of you.

   b. Step up and practice your half-volley hits.

   c. Ask your partner to mix up the tosses so that you can practice the shot from both your backhand and forehand sides. Try a two-handed grip if you need more control of the racket.

3. Get on a regular court. Practice these same strokes with tosses from a partner.

Drills for Drop Shot.

1. Get a racket in your hand and go through the motions of a drop shot.
2. Face a wall or fence about 6 to 10 feet away. Bounce a ball lightly in front of you and practice the drop-shot moves. Bounce the ball so that you can practice the shot from your backhand side.
3. Get on a court and stand several feet from the net. Bounce the ball near you and practice your drop shot so that the ball barely clears the net.
4. Get a partner on the other side of the net to make soft tosses to you.

Drills for Putting Spin on the Ball.

1. Without a racket, go through the motions of putting topspin or backspin on the ball. Go through the same motion with a racket.
2. Face a wall or fence about 3 to 5 yards back. Bounce a ball near you and practice the backspin or topspin with your bare hand. Move back a few more yards and try these skills with a racket.
3. Get on a court. Stand near the service line. Bounce a ball and try for a topspin or backspin hit that travels over the net.
4. Stand between the service line and the base line and have your partner stand on the other side of the net. Your partner makes easy tosses so you can practice putting backspin or topspin on your strokes.

8

The Doubles Game

Are you ready to choose a partner for a game of doubles? Will your teammate be a friend? Brother? Sister? Parent?

Who will serve first? Where will the player stand to make the serve? Where do other players move on the court when play begins? Which strokes are the most popular in the doubles game?

FANS ENJOY THE DOUBLES GAME

Tennis fans enjoy watching two evenly matched teams. The play action is speeded up because there are four players on the court instead of two to hit the ball. Oftentimes the fans will see not one, two, or three, but all four players moving close to the net. This kind of play usually starts a short rally with one player suddenly connecting for an overhead smash and a quick score.

There are some players who like the game of doubles better than they do the singles game. These players like the idea of playing with a friend as a teammate. They soon discover that certain strokes and strategies work better in doubles than they do in singles.

CHOOSING A PARTNER

The partner you choose as a teammate will depend upon the kind of pick-up game or tournament you enter. Here are some of the doubles team events that are sponsored.

1. Boys' doubles play
2. Girls' doubles play
3. Mixed doubles (one girl, one boy)
4. Husband-and-wife mixed doubles
5. Father-and-son doubles
6. Mother-and-daughter doubles
7. Brother-and-sister mixed doubles
8. Pro (professional)-amateur doubles

Try to select a partner who knows your playing habits or who can learn them quickly. It is possible that one teammate may be stronger than you in one part of the game and weaker in another. Each player must understand these differences and use the information to advantage during a game. It is also important that you play against a doubles team that is evenly matched with the talents of your team. You will have more exciting games when you follow these simple rules.

DIMENSIONS OF DOUBLES COURT

The doubles court is 36 feet wide, 9 feet wider than the singles court. A doubles sideline is added 4½ feet on the outside of each of the singles sidelines. The additional lines connect with both ends of the base lines. The area between the singles and doubles sidelines is called the *alley*. All remaining court dimensions remain the same as for the singles game.

RULES FOR DOUBLES

Rules for doubles and singles are almost the same. Some of the more important differences you will have to remember are:

1. After the serve is made, the players may hit the ball in any of the alley areas.
2. The same server must serve through an entire game.
3. If you serve during the first game, your partner serves through the third game. Your opponents will alternate serving during the second and fourth games.
4. Either partner is allowed to hit the ball after the receiver has returned the serve.
5. When you and your partner are trying to get the ball onto your opponents' court, only one stroke is allowed for your team.
6. The player receiving the service must continue to receive it on the same side until a set is over. After each set a team may change the order of receiving.

SKILLS FOR DOUBLES PLAY

The skills you use for singles are also used for doubles. The big difference is that certain ones are more useful in doubles than in singles.

In singles, most of the action takes place in the *backcourt.* In doubles, a lot of the action takes place in the *forecourt* (front court) or in the area closer to the net. Players depend more upon groundstrokes in singles, while in doubles they rely more on the volley and overhead smash shots.

The more you play doubles the faster you will discover when and which of these skills are used most often.

YOUR POSITION ON THE DOUBLES COURT

How do the players' court positions differ in doubles from those of players in singles game? During the serve? After the serve? Before answering these questions, you and your partner must consider two simple suggestions:

1. Each player on a team must find the best way to cover his or her portion of the court.
2. After play begins, both partners must find the best way for moving close to the net area. This puts both players in the best position to score points.

Partners Cover One-Half Court. The players *in singles* cover the full area on their side of the court. *In doubles,* each partner usually covers about one-half of his or her court. Normally, one player

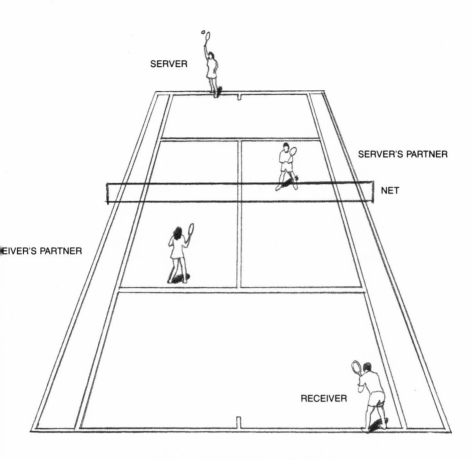

SERVER

SERVER'S PARTNER

NET

EIVER'S PARTNER

RECEIVER

PLAYER POSITIONS IN DOUBLES

covers the left side of the court and the partner plays the right side of the court. This means that you will divide your side of the court in two. You do this by drawing an imaginary line connecting the base-line center marker with the center service line.

This plan usually allows your partner and you to play side by side, each of you playing the ball on your own side of the court.

Serving-Team Position. When you serve in doubles, you should stand about halfway between the center marker and the doubles sideline. This position helps you defend against any return ball that travels toward either the alley or the center service line.

Your partner takes a ready position close to the net on the opposite side of your court. *The partner* should stand about 2 to 4 feet from the doubles sideline toward the center of the court. The distance from the net should be from 7 to 10 feet. This position keeps your partner from being hit by your serve. It also puts your partner in a good spot to cover an opponent's return of the serve.

Receiving-Team Position. When you *receive the ball* from the server, you should stand ready near the base line somewhere between the doubles sideline and the service marker. Put yourself in a diagonal line with the server. This splits your side of the court in two and gets you ready to make a forehand or backhand return stroke.

Your partner should stand ready on the opposite service line halfway between the doubles sideline and the center line. This position is just about in the middle of your partner's half court. It is the best spot for your partner to handle a ball hit on his or her side of the court.

See Chapter nine for information about *doubles tennis stragegy.*

HINTS FOR DOUBLES

1. Try to remember that you have a partner on

your side. Each of you must play as a member of a team.

2. Know your partner's strong and weak points. Give your partner the same information about yourself.
3. Concentrate on covering your portion of the court. Avoid trying to cover your partner's area, unless your partner gives you an emergency signal to do so.
4. After the serve, look for a chance to move in close to the net.
5. Try to keep your opponents in their backcourt by hitting deep.

DRILLS FOR DOUBLES

1. *For Two Players.* Both partners stand on the same side of the court. You act as the server while your partner takes the server's partner position near the net. Serve ten to twenty balls onto the empty opponent's service court.
   - Was your partner in the way of your serves?
   - Did you move forward toward the service area after the serve?
   - Was your partner ready to cover a ball hit just over the net?
   - Who would stroke a ball that lands between the two of you?

After each serve, you and your partner should practice the same movements that you would make during a real match. Change positions and give your partner a chance to serve.

2. *For Three Players.* You and your partner take the receiver's position on the court. Have a third player on the opponent's side of the court serve ten to twenty times onto your service court.
   - Were you able to return the serve into the opponent's backcourt?
   - Were you able to move toward the net after returning the serve?
   - Was your partner in a good position to return the ball with a volley or overhead smash if it was hit into his or her area?
   - Which partner had the stronger stroke to hit a ball traveling between the two of you?
   - Did you yell, "You take it," "Your ball," "Get it," or give some other signal to tell your partner to hit the ball?

3. *For Four Players.* Choose your partner and take positions on opposite sides of the court. One team starts by acting as the servers. The other team takes the position of the receivers. *No score is kept.* The idea is to give everyone the opportunity to practice.
   - Were players from the same team able to move toward the net to make some volley or smash shots?

- Were your strokes deep enough to keep your opponents in the backcourt?
- Did you get any lobs over your opponent's head when he or she played too close to the net?
- Were you able to return the serves directly to the server's backcourt, and not to the opponent's partner, who is close to the net?

Help each other by making up your own practice drills. See that each team gets a chance to be servers and receivers.

9

Tennis Strategy

The game is under way! The fans are excited! They are guessing how the players will use their skills. Players, coaches, and fans constantly read about how a singles player or doubles team "outfoxed," "outwitted," and "outplayed" their opponents. This is known as using game strategy. *Strategy* is the science of planning and directing your game. It also means that you use brain power in preparing an *advance plan of action* for a game against your opponent.

During a championship tournament, a top player said, "In the first set I wasn't playing my game. I changed my strategy in the second set and started hitting topspins. In the first set I was slicing the ball outside the sideline." This player had decided in advance to change her style of play if parts of her game weren't working. *Every competitor learns early that planning game action in advance brings out the best in a player.*

ONE PLAN WILL NOT ALWAYS WORK!

One plan of action will not work for all game situations. That's because your opponents do not always play alike. The court surfaces may differ. Or your style of play may change as you keep learning and improving. The important thing is to *study before a game.*

Train yourself to think quickly on your feet once the game starts. It's like spending extra time studying before you take a test in school. During the test, you try to *concentrate* on selecting the best answers to the questions. *Your best strategy for now is to depend upon the strokes you know well.* The next step is to study and practice the best way to use these strokes for the many different game situations that occur.

STRATEGY FOR ALL PLAYERS

Here are some simple rules that every player should follow:

1. Know the kind of court surface you will be using. Are the matches outdoors or indoors?
2. Warm up and practice some of your favorite strokes before starting a game.
3. Check to see if you can spot any of your

opponent's strong and weak points during the warm-up period.

4. Concentrate on your game and try not to argue or to let noises bother you.
5. Always use your best strokes against your opponent's weaknesses.
6. Try to keep the ball in play until you see an opening for a winning stroke. Try not to be forced into any errors. Let your opponent make the mistakes.
7. After every stroke, get yourself back into the best ready position for the next shot.

STRATEGY FOR SINGLES PLAYERS

Study these strategy points when you are preparing for a singles game.

1. Check to see if your opponent likes to play more of a net game or a base line game.
2. If your opponent plays close to the net, use the lob, an angled crosscourt shot, or a shot aimed directly at the feet.
3. If your opponent plays a base-line game, try using some short crosscourt or drop shots just over the net.
4. Keep the ball close to your opponent's base line until you get a chance for a winning point.
5. Force your opponent to run from one side to the other with good sideline and crosscourt shots. This is known as keeping your opponent "on the run."

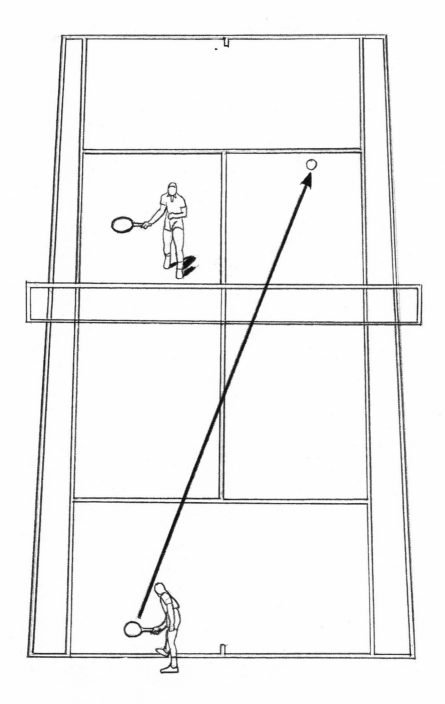

SCORING POINT ON BACKHAND CROSSCOURT SHOT

6. Keep your opponent on the run with short and deep shots. Be careful that your opponent does not smash your short shots for points.
7. If you are forced into a defensive position, use the lob to move your opponent into the backcourt and away from the net.
8. Know when to be aggressive on offense. The first serve and volley are two good aggressive shots. A good, hard, first serve will allow you to move swiftly toward the net for a possible put-away volley shot.
9. Don't try to go for a quick "surprise score" when you return a first hard serve from your opponent.
10. Concentrate on returning your opponent's first serve as safely as possible to the backcourt. If the second serve is weak, you may try to use an aggressive shot by moving forward and forcing your opponent into a defensive position.

STRATEGY FOR DOUBLES PLAYERS

These are some of the more important strategy points you must be ready to use in the doubles game.

1. Partners must agree on the signals that will be used during the game. You could yell, "Mine," "Yours," "Take it," or "Get it." Hand signals are also used for some plays.
2. Help one another in calling balls that may

HAVE YOUR SIGNALS READY!
WHO HITS THE BALL?

land out-of-bounds by yelling "Out."

3. Try to keep the ball deep in your opponent's backcourt. This will allow you and your partner to move closer to the net for quick shots that score points.

4. Standing side by side about 15 feet from the net in your side of the court is the strongest offensive position for you and your partner.

5. Whichever partner is serving or receiving the ball should try to get up to the net with the other partner. This puts you in the side-by-side ready position.

6. If your opponents are overpowering you

by getting to the net first and scoring most of the points, a change in your style of play is called for. *Both* you and your partner change by starting to stand back near the base line. When the situation improves, you may return to the most popular offensive style by having one player closer to the net.

7. When your opponents insist on playing close to the net at all times, try lobbing over their heads. This helps to force them back toward the base line.

8. If a ball goes over your head, your partner, who is back, should go after the ball to make a return shot. At the same time, you should switch into the playing area left free by your partner.

9. A ball traveling between the two partners should usually be taken by the player in position for a strong forehand shot. Partners may yell, "Mine," "Yours," or "Take it" in this situation.

10. Partners should encourage one another. Avoid finding fault when a partner makes an error. Be patient and work as a team.

READY FOR THE NEXT SHOT?

After every stroke, you must move swiftly into the best court position to handle the next shot. Many beginning players make the mistake of standing still where they last hit the ball. Make it a habit of taking the position from which you can best cover the angle of your opponent's return. Remember these points:

1. Never stand and wait in the area between the base line and the service line. This is often called "no man's land," and it is a poor place to be.
2. Try moving into a center ready position on the court. Never stand off to one side of the court or remain still where you last hit the ball.
3. Study the angle of bounce of your opponent's ball as it approaches you. Gauge your distance so you *do not charge* into the ball at the point at which it bounces. Position yourself early so you won't be rushed, and you will have time to take your best relaxed stroke. THIS MEANS PRACTICE YOUR FOOTWORK.

WANT TO BE MORE AGGRESSIVE?

Here is an advanced skill for young players who wish to improve their aggressive style of play on offense. It is known as *approaching the net.* Here is an example:

1. Send a forehand or backhand stroke deep, to your opponent's base line.
2. Dash to the service line and hold that position.
3. Volley your opponent's next return by plac-

ing the shot safely but not going all out for a "winner" just yet.

4. Immediately after this volley, move a few steps closer to the net. This is known as your place to be to return your opponent's next hit.

5. From this spot you are ready to put the ball away rapidly for a point with your favorite shot.

Additional Hint. On the serve and during play, think of the approach to the net in three stages.

1. Stage one starts you at your base line.

2. Stage two moves you from base line to service line.

3. Stage three moves you from service line to within 10 or 15 feet of the net.

One last pointer: Always stop and plant your feet when you are about to volley. Never hit as you are running. These movements all require practice.

10

Equipment

Tennis is a game. Young players can have a good time playing against a wall, on a playground, and on an open field or vacant lot with flat ground. Boys and girls can get a good workout with just a racket, a ball, and a pair of sneakers.

Top amateur and professional players require more equipment because they play in championship tournaments. This equipment is needed for fast-action tennis, so that neither player nor team has an advantage during a match.

PERSONAL EQUIPMENT

The players' uniforms consist of jerseys (shirt or blouse), shorts or skirt, sneakers, socks, and head and wrist bands which help to absorb the player's perspiration from the forehead and wrists. The headband is also worn to keep long hair from covering the player's eyes during play.

PLAYERS IN FULL TENNIS DRESS

Official Ball. The tennis ball must be stitchless and between 2½ inches and 2⅝ inches in diameter. They must weigh more than 2 ounces and less than 2¹⁄₁₆ ounces. They are usually white, yellow, orange, or green. The balls are packed in sealed cans for protection. Balls are often designed specifically for competition indoors or outdoors, or for different types of tennis-court floors.

Racket. The tennis racket is the most important tool that a tennis player has. Just like a carpenter or doctor, a tennis player must keep the tools in good condition. Racket frames are made of wood, metal, fiber glass, aluminum, and graphite. Most strings are made of braided gut or nylon. A beginning player should seek the advice of a coach or teaching professional before selecting a racket. The weight, balance, and "grip feel" of the racket are important to each player.

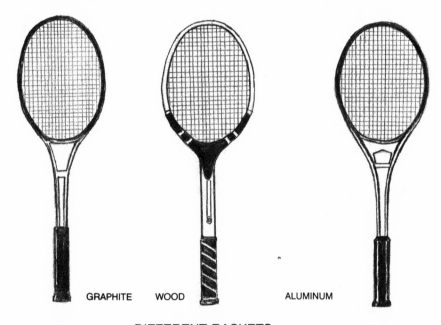

GRAPHITE   WOOD   ALUMINUM

DIFFERENT RACKETS

Racket Press and Cover. The *racket press* is placed over the head portion of a wooden racket. Screws on the racket press are tightened until it presses against both sides of the racket frame to prevent it from warping. The *racket cover* is made of cloth, canvas, or vinyl, and looks like a large pocket with a zipper on one side. It helps to protect the racket strings and frame.

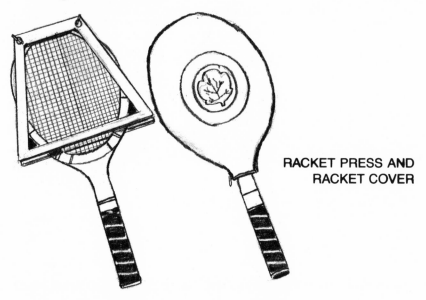

RACKET PRESS AND
RACKET COVER

OFFICIALS AND THEIR EQUIPMENT

For your everyday games you will not need officials. You rely on each player to tell the truth, to play fairly, and to practice "tennis courtesy" throughout a game. But did you know that as many as thirteen officials are on duty for championship matches? That each is located at a specific spot near the court? And that each has a different duty to perform? The thirteen officials in charge of a championship match are:

1. One referee
2. One umpire

3. One net umpire
4. Two center service linespeople
5. Four side linespeople
6. Two base linespeople
7. Two service linespeople

Referee. The referee has full control of the game. This official carries a rule book with which to settle arguments, if necessary. He or she sees that all other officials carry out their duties properly and that *all officials* wear clothing that is neat and of a dark color. During important matches the referee sits beside the court, alongside the umpire's chair.

Umpire (on elevated stand). This umpire is seated on a stand 5 to 7 feet high, located about 5 feet from one end of the net. The elevated position helps the umpire to see all the play action and the conduct of the other officials. The umpire has a scorecard and keeps score of the match. At the end of each match, the umpire signs the official scorecard and presents it to the authorities of the tournament.

Net Umpire. With one finger on the net, the net umpire sits near the net post in front of the umpire on the high perch. This official must be on the alert to call out the plays that occur at the net. The net umpire quickly yells out whether the play is a service "let," "fault," or "out." The net official also assists the other umpire by keeping a duplicate score of the match.

1. NET UMPIRE   2. ELEVATED UMPIRE POSITION

NET OFFICIALS STAND

Linespeople. These officials are also called linesmen, lineswomen, or linespeople. Ten work during championship matches. They must have good eyesight and the ability to concentrate on their duties. Each one is assigned to watch a specific court line during the action. They are seated off court facing the line assigned to them. During play, they must remain silent, and always alert to get out of a player's path if their sitting position will interfere with a stroke. It's important for these officials always to *watch the court line* and not the ball during the action. Here are some of the more specific duties of these officials:

Service Linespeople. There are two service linespeople. Each takes an off-court position *facing* one of the *court service lines.* If the ball on the serve lands behind the service line, it is up to these officials to call a "fault."

Center Service Linespeople. There are two center-service linespeople. Each takes a position *facing the net* well behind one of the base lines, directly in line with the center service line. They call a "foot fault" if the server is standing on the wrong side of the center-service mark, or a "fault" if the serve lands on the wrong side of the center service line.

Base Linespeople. There are two base linespeople. They *sit directly in line with one of the base lines.* These officials call a "foot fault" on the server when the foot-fault rule is broken.

Side Linespeople. There are four side linespeople. Each one is located well behind the base lines and *directly in line with one end of the sidelines.* They call a "foot fault" if the server is not standing on the correct side of the sideline, and a "fault" if a served ball lands outside of the singles sideline.

Ball Boys and Girls. Many youngsters like to have the job of ball boy or girl at championship matches. They are positioned just outside the playing court and they have a chance to watch the action and also to meet and talk to many of the players. These young boys and girls help the referee and umpire to speed up the game. Most wear clothing similar to a tennis player's. One or two take a low kneeling position just behind each net post. Three to six other young boys and girls are located well behind the two base lines. The duty of the ball boys and girls is to retrieve or chase all loose tennis balls that are hit and end up out of the player's reach. The idea is to go after loose balls with speed, quickly leave the court area, and go back to a kneeling position. If players request an extra ball, a ball boy or girl gives it to them. It's important for ball boys and girls to remain silent when play is in progress.

FIELD EQUIPMENT

A tennis court has a rectangular shape. It is marked with white lines. The size of the court changes with the singles or doubles game. (See page 17 for the exact dimensions.)

Tennis Posts. A heavy-duty steel post is placed 3 feet outside of each sideline. Attached to each post is a *ratchet reel with a handle* to help keep the net tight at all times.

Tennis Nets. Tennis nets come in singles or doubles-game lengths. They are made of flexible steel, aluminum mesh wire, weatherproof polyethylene, nylon, and other synthetic fibers.

Tennis Band. This is also known as a *headband.* The headband is attached along the entire length of the net at the top. It is made of nylon, canvas, or other strong materials. The color is usually white so it can be seen easily by the players.

Tennis Strap. The strap is also called a *center strap.* It is a 2-inch-wide strip of nylon or canvas wrapped around the very center of the net. Here the net must measure 3 feet high instead of the 3½ feet it measures at the posts.

Cables. A strong cable slides inside the headband that is along the top of the net. The ends of the cable are then attached to the ratchet reel of each post so that the net can be tightened. Cables are made of steel, nylon, or polyethylene rope.

Players' Bench. The players' bench is usually behind the elevated umpire stand and just in front of the spectator stands. Fresh fruit juices, water, towels, and players' additional tennis rackets are located nearby.

Scoreboard. Scoreboards are found in different locations depending on whether the game is played indoors or outdoors. Most tournaments provide at least one large scoreboard where it can be seen by all the fans. Large facilities have one scoreboard above each end of the spectator stands. They show the names of the players, games played, and sets won and lost.

Backstops and Sidestops. These pieces of equipment surround the area on all four sides of the court. Positioned directly in front of the first row of seats, they prevent tennis balls from landing in the spectator stands. Backstops and sidestops are made of fine wood, mesh wire or mesh nylon fencing, or canvas curtain.

Choice Seats. All fans would like seats close to the court area. These are the choicest seats. Of course everyone can't have a seat near the court. So whether you have one of these prize seats or must watch the matches from the top spectator row, you can still have fun at the matches and cheer for your favorite.

PRACTICE EQUIPMENT FOR EVERYONE

Many schools, parks, and tennis clubs have special equipment for beginners and advanced players to practice their tennis skills. Three of the most popular are:

1. Automatic serving-striking machine
2. Rebound net
3. Rebound cord and ball

The *automatic serving-striking machine* can be used when you have no one to practice with. The machine can be adjusted to hit a ball toward you at up to 90 miles per hour. It allows you to practice your backhand or forehand drives, cross-court shots, lobs, overhead smashes, drop shots, and many other shots. The machine can give you a ball with topspin, backspin, or with no spin. You can practice shots from a stationary or running position. Both beginners and professionals can use the machine.

The *rebound tennis net* is a portable piece of equipment with a nylon net about 9 feet high and 12 feet wide. The net is attached to a metal frame and stand. The net can be tilted to adjust the speed and angle of the rebound ball, or for practicing volley, overhead smashes, serves, and groundstrokes. It does not require a lot of space and can be used by two players at the same time.

The *rebound cord and ball* is a piece of equipment that can be used almost any time and anywhere. A ball is attached to one end of a long rubber cord, which is fastened at the opposite end to a stake driven into the ground. Or, for indoor or outdoor use, the cord may be attached to a heavy, padded, flat base of steel or wood.

11

Getting Ready for the Big Match

At last! Your team is going to play against another team!

This is not only exciting, it is a very valuable experience. After the game is over, the players are able to judge just how well they played. Each player and each team can recognize weak spots in the playing and will know what to practice in order to improve.

What must you know to prepare for a match? Is the competition open to anyone? Are only certain age groups allowed to play? Where are the matches going to be held? Are you going to have teams made up of both boys and girls? Do the rules allow for singles, doubles, and mixed-doubles games? Is there a competent umpire? What about linespeople and ball boys and girls? Do you have a captain?

These and many more questions must be answered before the tennis competition starts. Of course, it is most important for each boy and girl to be physically fit and trained before the day of the matches.

KEEPING PHYSICALLY FIT

As you prepare for a game or series of matches, you should be healthy and strong. Top players know their training rules and obey them. So should you. The rules are simple:

1. Get a proper amount of sleep. This may take will power, especially when there is a late TV show you don't want to miss.
2. Get plenty of fresh air and exercise. Play outdoor games.
3. Eat good, nourishing food every day. Learn to eat foods like milk, eggs, vegetables, and cheese. These foods help the bones, muscles, and body grow bigger and stronger.
4. Bathe or shower regularly.
5. Brush your teeth after meals.
6. Take care of cuts and scratches right away. If you feel sick, don't hide it.
7. Do not neglect your studies while you are in training.

Follow these rules. Top players do.

CHOOSING A COURT

Where are you going to play? Is it going to be an indoor or an outdoor game?

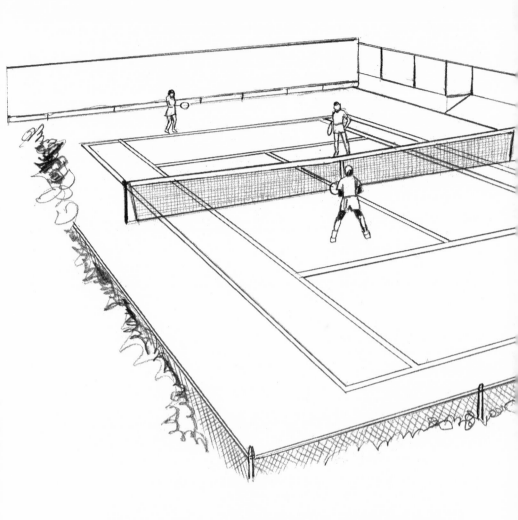

Indoor tennis games require a school, club, or park gymnasium. Outdoor tennis usually requires courts found on the carefully maintained grounds at a school, park, or private club. Most regulation indoor and outdoor tennis courts are not available for younger competitors. *Do not let the lack of facilities and equipment stop you from competing.* But be sure to find a safe place. If you can use an official court, fine; if not, ask your parents, teachers, and coaches for makeshift tennis courts that can be substituted.

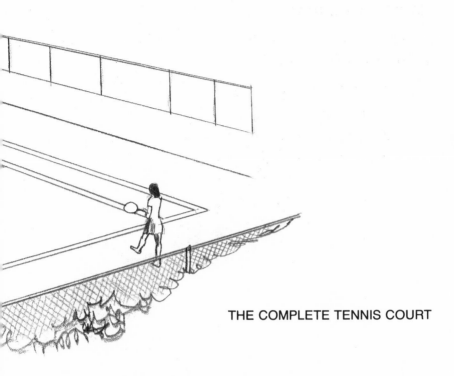

THE COMPLETE TENNIS COURT

Once you've found a place to play, the following things must be done before the competition begins.

CHECKING THE COURT AND NET

Your court must be a safe place to play.

Get a good broom and sweep loose trash and dust off the court and surrounding area. Place the refuse in a box and carry it away to a larger trash container.

Check to see if the tennis-court markings are available for both singles and doubles game. Have a ruler or tape measure ready. Does the exact center of the net measure 3 feet high from the ground? Is it 3 feet 6 inches high at each post?

EQUIPMENT AND SUPPLIES

Here is a list of supplies that may help you to get ready for a big tournament.

1. Rule book.
2. Medical service and first-aid kit.
3. Score book and scorecards.
4. List of officials.
5. List of players entered in the different events (age-group, singles, doubles, mixed-doubles events).
6. Ruler or measuring tape.
7. Pencils and pads of paper.
8. Additional tennis balls and rackets.
9. Broom to keep the court area clean.
10. Players' bench or chairs.
11. High perch or stand for the umpire. Use a high stool if a regulation stand is not available.
12. Chairs for other officials.
13. Ball boys and girls.
14. *Scoreboard.* Use old lumber and cardboard to make one large, portable scoreboard so players and fans can see it. The scoreboard should show:

   • the names of players
   • the game scores for each set.

Example:

NAMES	GAMES AND SETS				
Tony	6	4	6	3	6
Bobby	3	6	2	6	2

HAVING FUN WITHOUT FULL UNIFORMS

YOUNG PLAYERS' PERSONAL EQUIPMENT

Never allow a lack of equipment to keep you from playing. Wear your school gym clothes or anything comfortable, but make sure the soles of your sneakers are the type allowed on the court where you'll be playing.

Do not purchase an expensive racket, balls, or clothing without the advice of your teacher, coach, or parent.

GAME OFFICIALS

Captain. Each team selects a captain. This player should be liked and respected by all the members of the team. If an argument comes up, the captain represents the team. A captain settles disputes with the referee or umpire or with the captain of the opposing team.

Coach. In an important tournament, an older person should act as coach. This person makes all the substitutions and decides who will play in the singles and doubles matches. The coach sees that the team plays the game according to the rules. If there is no coach, the captain takes care of these duties.

Scorekeeper. The umpire on the high stand acts as the scorekeeper. All scorecards should be saved because they are the only records of the team's work. The scorecards for each team and match show the names of players, score of the games, and the number of sets won and lost.

If a team wants a more nearly complete record, the players and official scorekeeper should refer to Chapter Twelve, "Scores and Records," for additional information.

Referee and Umpire. A grownup should act as referee or umpire for an important tournament. This person should know tennis well. It could be your teacher, a parent, an older student, or a member of some local tennis club.

This official must be fair in making decisions. But sometimes game officials do make mistakes. When this happens there is little you can do. The referee's or umpire's word is final.

Linespeople. Older students who are fair and know tennis could act as linespeople. They must work closely with the referee or umpire.

Ball Boys and Girls. Young students can be assigned these duties. They should be fast on their feet to retrieve loose balls and always have enough balls on hand for the server.

ARRANGING FOR A GAME

Making arrangements for a tennis tournament is a big job. Many details must be attended to well ahead of time. The coach, the captain, or the boy or girl selected as team secretary can make the arrangements in any of these ways:

1. They phone the captain or coach of the other team and ask to play against them.
2. They write a letter asking for playing dates.
3. They visit the other captain or coach and plan the details of the tournament.

Make sure that the other team players are a fair match for yours. Teams should be matched as to grade in school, playing ability, and experience. If you compete against players that are much heavier, bigger, and more experienced, the matches will probably be one-sided. Also, you must decide how many singles, doubles, and mixed-doubles matches will be played.

The captain, coach, or team secretary should

keep a written record of the matches to be played. This record should show:

1. Where the matches will be played (indoors or outdoors).
2. The names of the players on each team.
3. The exact rules that will be followed (boys' or girls' only, some of each, or mixed doubles).
4. Number of games and sets played by each player.
5. The final player and team scores.
6. The officials of the match.
7. The equipment owned by each team.

After all the arrangements are made, give your teammates as much information as possible about the matches they will play.

It's quite a job getting ready for a big match. Now you have a slight idea of what goes on behind the scenes in a school, college, or big-league tennis club; letters, telegrams, contracts, meetings, and many, many worries. Right now, your worries are on a much smaller scale. The important thing to remember is that you are playing tennis because it's fun and you enjoy the game.

MORE HELP GETTING STARTED

The *United States Tennis Association* (USTA) is ready to help you start a beginner's tennis club close to where you live. They developed a *Starter Tennis Skill Test* for beginners. The different tests can be practiced in a schoolyard, on the blacktop, against a wall, or in a gymnasium. Another program the USTA developed is *Courtstar*. This is a brand-new, on-court instructional program for young players. Ask your parents, teacher, or coach to help you get the information about these programs.* These organizations are out to help you! Try them!

*Write to USTA, Education and Research Center, 729 Alexander Road, Princeton, New Jersey 08540.

12

Scores and Records

You and your friends get a report card from school that tells you how well you are doing. Did you know that tennis players also receive report cards? Their report cards may look different from the one you get at school, but the cards serve a purpose very much like yours. They show how well the players do their work. How is a tennis player's report card made out? Who prepares the cards? Who figures the player's marks and rates the team's performance?

The record really begins when you start to study and practice for a game. It continues on the tennis court with the work of the umpire and other game officials. Every time you score or commit a fault it becomes part of your record. Not many fans see the tremendous amount of material that is collected by officials and coaches who help to prepare the final report.

OFFICIAL SCOREKEEPER

There is an official scorekeeper for all important tennis matches. This official is also the umpire who sits on a high stand at one side of the net. The scorekeeper knows the tennis rules and understands the skills of the players. On large sheets of paper, the scorekeeper answers many questions about each team and its players. Some of these questions are answered on the *official tennis game program,* which shows the players' names, ages, weights, heights, towns, schools, and past records. But most important, the scorekeeper must have ready a *master game-scoring sheet.*

In different areas around the court and stands, there may be reporters from college, school, and community newspapers, as well as radio and TV announcers. They also follow the game closely and keep their own scores and records.

PLAYER RECORDS

These are some of the more important bits of information the scorekeeper records for each player during the game:

1. Which player served first.
2. Number of points scored by each player in each game.
3. Number of games won by each player in each set.
4. Number of sets won by each player in a match or tournament.

5. Number of faults each player committed.
6. Length of each game, set, and match.

TEAM RECORDS

These are some of the more important team matters the scorekeepers will report on during the matches:

1. Name and team rank of each player.
2. Name of team player serving and receiving first.
3. Name of player scoring most team points.
4. Name of team scoring most points, winning most games and sets, and winning the match.
5. Length of each team's matches.

TEAM SCOREKEEPER

Each team also has its own scorekeeper. This person may be the coach, manager, or someone else who knows the game of tennis. These school or club scorekeepers keep an even more detailed record of the players. For every player a record of this added information is kept:

1. Was the player steady during the game?
2. In the doubles game, was the player on the move to help a teammate? Was there teamwork?
3. What percentage of first serves were good?
4. Did the player commit any foot faults?

5. Did the player use the proper stances and strokes?
6. Did the player tire easily?
7. Did the player argue with the officials?
8. Was the player injured during the match?
9. Did the player show better defensive or offensive work?

Most teams also have team secretaries or managers. After each game, the official scorekeeper (umpire) gives a report to managers or secretaries of each team. Copies of the report are then sent to the league or conference commissioner. This commissioner sees that the records are kept as lasting accounts of the games.

Tennis teams, clubs, conferences, and associations have offices where these records are also kept. Coaches study them to investigate the weak and strong points of their players. *Then all players are rated on ability and skill.* That's why these records are so important.

PLAYERS STUDY THE RECORDS

The coach posts portions of these records in the players' dressing or meeting room so they may be studied. Players may ask for individual copies so they can study their own records more carefully. Like a teacher, the coach studies these reports to help each player and the team improve.

Many times some of this information is also printed in the daily newspapers a day or two before the matches.

SOUVENIR TENNIS PROGRAM

Before big matches, fans usually buy programs. These look like magazines and provide a great deal of information. They give the names of the players entered in the tournament, and their heights, weights, and ages.

The order in which the players are scheduled to play is selected from the list of players printed in the official tennis program. The program also lists the team records, and players' records and their home towns.

Here is a *sample line-up of players* who are entered in an invitational tournament. The line-up shows that the *seeded* players have a number circled after their names. The number tells the fans the order in which certain players are ranked as the best in the competition. The best players are seeded so they will not compete against one another in the early rounds.

FIGURING PERCENTAGE

The best place to figure percentage is in school. *Percentage helps you to figure out the team and player ratings.* From the percentages shown in the newspapers, fans also can learn:

1. The players' and team's standing in the league, conference, country, or world.
2. Each player's won, lost record in the singles, doubles, and mixed-doubles game.
3. Each player's serving accuracy.

SAMPLE LINE-UP AND GAME SCHEDULE

FIRST ROUND MATCHES	QUARTERFINAL ROUND	SEMIFINAL ROUND	FINAL ROUND
(Weds., Thurs.)	*(Winners of 1st Round)*	*(Winners of Quarterfinal)*	*(Winners of Semifinal)*

1. Claude (two), France

2. Terry, Australia

    Friday

3. Cliff, So. Africa

4. Jaime, Mexico

    Saturday

5. Ulf (four), Sweden

6. Carlos, Brazil

    Friday

7. Jorge (six), Chile

8. Peter, Yugoslavia

    Sunday   Champion

9. Juan, Puerto Rico

10. Gerald, Australia

    Friday

11. Milan, Canada

12. Bernardo (five), Italy

    Saturday

13. Bob (three), G. Britain

14. Brian, U.S.A.

    Friday

15. Arnold, W. Germany

16. Allan (one), U.S.A.

4. The players' scoring average on offensive and defensive shots.

To figure the "team" percentage, or standing, in the league or conference, *take the number of matches won and divide by the number of matches played.*

> *Example:* The Panthers have played twenty-two matches. They won eighteen matches and lost four. What is the Panthers' percentage, or standing, in the league?
>
> $$22 \sqrt{\overline{18.000}} = .818 = \text{team percentage in the league}$$

To figure the percentage of matches won by a player, the problem is worked a little differently. Take the number of matches won, divide by the number of matches played, then move the decimal point two places to the right.

> *Example:* Barbie won twelve matches out of eighteen matches played. What was her winning percentage?
>
> $$18 \sqrt{\overline{12.000}} = .666$$

To change a decimal to percentage, move the decimal point two places to the right.

Your answer will be: 66.6 (sixty-six and six-tenths) is Barbie's winning average.

SAMPLE SCORE SHEET

Here is one of the many different kinds of score sheets used by teams and players:

SAMPLE TENNIS SCORE SHEET

DATE _____ HOLIDAY TOURNAMENT PLAYERS' INITIALS

Games Played	Server's Initials	SET No. 1 _____ POINTS	Games Won M.A.	Won B.C.
1	M.A.	1 1 1 1 / 1 1	1	0
2	B.C.	1 1 1 1 1 1 1 / 1 1 1 1 1	1	1
3	M.A.	1 1 1 1 / 1 1	2	1
4	B.C.	1 1 1 1 / 1 1	2	2
5	M.A.	1 1 1 1 / 1	3	2
6	B.C.	1 1 1 / 1 1 1 1 1	4	2
7	M.A.	1 1 1 1 1 / 1 1 1	5	2
8	B.C.	1 / 1 1 1 1	6	2
9				
10				

WON BY _____ M.A. _____ SCOREKEEPER _____

SCORE _____ 6–2 _____ PLACE __Memorial Tennis Courts__

157

NOTE: Only the initials of the server appear in the boxes. Points scored by the server are always marked in the top row of the small boxes. Points of the receiver are always marked in the bottom row of boxes. The score sheet shows that *M.A. won the first game* by scoring the following points: 15–love, 30–love, 30–15, 40–15, 40–30, and game. The *second game was won by B.C.* with the following scores: love–15, 15–all, 15–30, 30–all, 40–30, deuce, ad in, deuce, ad out, deuce, ad in, and game. The remaining games show that the winner of the first set was M.A. (See Chapter Two for more nearly complete rules of scoring.)

GAME RESULTS

Throughout the tennis tournament the results of the matches are printed in the daily newspapers. Reporters write a running account of the matches, leading scorers, team standings, and many more statistics and records. A great number of today's top players made a note of their own records when they were younger. They kept using these records to study their game. Put the important statistics and records in your *tennis notebook.* It will help you improve your play as you continue to grow bigger and stronger.

Here is one way that the results of a tennis tournament appear in the sports pages.

FINAL ROUND

Men's Singles
Jimmy (Illinois) defeated Ken (Australia) 6–1, 6–1, 6–4.

Men's Doubles
John & Tony (Australia) defeated Stan (S.C.) & Bob (Calif.) 8–6, 6–4, 6–4.

Women's Singles
Chris (Florida) defeated Rita (Brazil) 6–4, 3–6, 6–2.

Women's Doubles
Peggy (Calif.) & Evonne (Australia) defeated Helen & Karen (Australia) 2–6, 6–4, 6–3.

Mixed Doubles
Billy Jean (S.C.) & Owen (Australia) defeated Lesley & Mark (Britain) 6–3, 9–7.

Junior Boys
Billy (N.Y.) defeated Ashok (India) 6–2, 6–3.

Junior Girls
Marina (France) defeated Mariana (Britain) 6–4, 6–4.

The newspapers also print the standings of each school and college team, or professional league.

YOUTH TENNIS LEAGUE STANDINGS

NORTH DIVISION

	W	L	Pct.	MB
Freedoms	18	4	.818	. . .
Beavers	14	11	.560	5½
Violets	8	15	.348	10½
Wildcats	7	17	.292	12

SOUTH DIVISION

	W	L	Pct.	MB
Majorettes	17	8	.680	. . .
Panthers	17	8	.680	. . .
Horsemen	16	8	.667	½
Troopers	7	18	.280	10

EAST DIVISION

	W	L	Pct.	MB
Eagles	15	9	.625	. . .
Bisons	13	9	.591	1
Vikings	12	14	.462	4
Trojans	10	15	.400	5½

WEST DIVISION

	W	L	Pct.	MB
Diplomats	13	11	.542	. . .
Warriors	11	12	.478	1½
Rams	12	14	.462	2
Badgers	4	21	.160	9½

Key to figures: W means matches won. L means matches lost. Pct. means percentage of matches won. MB means matches behind. These records and others show how each player performed in all the games during the tennis season.

How did you do? How did your team perform? Your opponents'? Check with your friends and examine your own records. Ask your parents or teacher to help you figure percentages and averages if you need help. Then work on the game skills in which you show weaknesses.

For the big-league teams, men and women sit at desks all through the tennis season and work on figures and percentages. This work results in the scores and records that make up tennis history.

13

Your Manners on the Court

How players act and behave on and off the court is an important part of the game of tennis. From the time of the introduction of the game into Europe and America, players have followed certain *manners and customs* known as etiquette when playing tennis. Many are not included in the official rules of tennis. But throughout the years, players, officials, and fans have accepted these manners and customs as part of the game.

Whether you have a pick-up game with a friend or take part in a tournament, see that your conduct is good. Here are some rules and suggestions that will help make the game more enjoyable for you, your friends, opponents, and fans.

BEFORE THE GAME

1. Learn the more important rules of tennis. Study Chapter Two, *Know Your Tennis,* for

a better understanding of the game. It will prevent possible embarrassment to you and those around you.

2. If you plan to play just with friends, agree ahead of time how the game rules will be enforced. This means that each player must take on the duties of a linesperson *and* scorekeeper.

3. If you play in a tournament, introduce yourself to your opponent before the match.

4. See if the center height of the net is 36 inches.

5. Agree with the other players about the length of the warm-up period. They usually last from 5 to 10 minutes. Ask your partner or opponent if he or she wishes to practice warm-up strokes with you.

6. Check who will spin the racket or toss a coin to decide the choice of serve and side of court.

7. Wear tennis shoes and clean, comfortable clothing for your friendly pick-up games. Dress rules for official tournaments usually require that you wear a T-shirt or blouse, shorts or skirt, and tennis shoes.

DURING A MATCH

1. When you practice or rally with a friend, respect the other players on the courts next to you.

2. Once on the court, keep your voice down.

Don't be rowdy. Concentrate on your game.

3. In a real match, obey the decisions of the officials. If you disagree with a call, ask for an explanation *after* the match.

4. If there are no officials, the players must officiate at the match. This calls for each player to take on the duties of the linesperson and scorekeeper.

   a. You must call all line plays on your side of the net. Your opponent calls all line plays on the opposite side of the net.

   b. If you *clearly* see a ball go outside the line on your opponent's side, you must call it "out" against yourself. If you don't actually see your opponent's ball go "out" on your side of the net, you call it "in." It's a point for your opponent.

   c. Help the other player make a decision only when asked.

   d. Do not serve until your opponent is ready. It is not fair to make a serve to catch your opponent off guard. The server must call out the score before serving each point.

   e. The receiver of the serve should immediately call a "let" if a ball was served before the receiver was ready. This calls for the point to be played over.

f. The receiver should not return a serve that is known to be out of the service court. A loud "out" should be called instantly if the receiver could not avoid making a return swing on a ball just outside the line.

g. If a ball from another court interferes with your play, stop and quickly call a "let" and start the play over.

h. The server should not take advantage of making a foot fault when serving. It is unfair and careless if you don't call a "foot fault" just because your opponent cannot see the error.

i. Volunteer to make calls against yourself when you touch or reach over the net, when you hit the ball after two bounces, when you make a double-hit to get the ball over the net, or when the ball touches your clothing.

5. Never pull or lean against the net even when play has stopped.

6. Return a ball from another court only after a point is over.

7. Do not run after your ball if it goes onto another player's court. Wait until their point is over and politely thank them for returning the ball.

8. Older players usually have two tennis balls in one hand during the serve. This helps to speed up the game if the first serve is not good. If your hand is too small to hold two

tennis balls, keep a second ball in one of your pockets.

9. During *doubles play,* the receiver's partner should make the service-line calls. Both the receiver and partner make the calls at the center and sidelines of the service court.

10. Partners should not delay the game with long conversations on the court. They may, however, encourage one another with such kind and helpful words as "nice going," "my ball," "out," "yours."

11. Shake hands with your opponent at the end of every match.

IF YOU ARE A FAN!

Whether you are a fan watching a pick-up match or a championship tournament, here are some suggestions that will help you become a "top notch" spectator.

1. Do nothing that will bother the players' game concentration.

2. Show consideration for the players. Don't make distracting movements and loud noises while play is going on. *Ask yourself how you would want people to act while you are playing in a match.*

3. Do not ask out loud for a score until after a point is announced.

4. Accept the decisions of the game officials.

**SHAKE HANDS
AT END OF MATCH**

5. Never move around from seat to seat, rattle paper, or wave at a friend during the play for a point.
6. Avoid entering the court, or walking across or behind a court until a game is over.
7. Applaud a great play only after the point is completed.
8. Applaud both players after a match for playing their best.

Following these courtesies and customs will let you enjoy the game of tennis just as the top players, coaches, and fans do.

14

For the Interested Person
Who Can't Play

The weak, the strong, the young, the old! It makes no difference: *Tennis can be enjoyed by everyone.* Many stories are written about great athletes who were sick or suffered serious accidents or illnesses when they were young.

How did many of these people become successful in later life? Much of their success was possible because they kept physically active in the best way they knew how. Some read sports books; others talked to great tennis players and coaches and worked hard to strengthen their bodies. Later on as neighborhood, school, and college athletes, they won high-ranking tennis honors. *Many well-known people could not play tennis for one reason or another.* But this did not stop them from taking part in other ways and enjoying the game.

IF YOU CAN'T PLAY TENNIS

Before young boys and girls go out for tennis, they should get permission from their parents. *They should also be examined by a doctor.* Sometimes a doctor will not allow a person to take part in active sports. So, if you can't play tennis, don't feel sorry for yourself. There are many ways in which you can still take part and enjoy the game.

Follow the Game. Follow the tennis action on TV and radio. Read about tennis in books, magazines, and newspapers.

Help Arrange for Games. Find the right team for your club to compete against. Be a team secretary. Keep the team records.

Assist the Scorekeeper. Help the scorekeeper with the score book and records of your team. Write a report of what every player does on the court. Figure out playing records and percentages.

Be a Reporter. Help with the publicity for your team. Make posters and signs to advertise when and where your team will compete. Report the games to the school and neighborhood newspapers.

Help Take Care of Equipment. Help arrange for the supplies and equipment your team needs. Help check correct height of net and cleanliness of the court area.

Be a Referee's or Umpire's Assistant. Help to officiate at a game by acting as a linesperson.

Be a Coach's Assistant. Record the names of the team players before game time. Help print forms for strategy plays and training rules. This is usually done on an office printing machine.

Be a Player's Practice Assistant. Help a team player to practice. Find a safe spot and toss tennis balls so members of the team can practice different strokes.

Practicing Yourself. Are there some skills you wish to practice by yourself? With friends? Or with your family? After you decide what you would like to do, talk it over with your parents. They may wish to ask the doctor if you may do what you have chosen. Have your list of drills ready to show the doctor, so a decision can be made on which ones are allowed.

There are quite a lot of ways you can be active. Whether you are blind, deaf, in a wheelchair, or have other disabilities, find out about the kind of programs that are right for you. There are organizations for the physically handicapped, as well as the Joseph P. Kennedy, Jr., foundation for the mentally retarded, that sponsor sports and fitness activities for youngsters. The United States Tennis Association (USTA) has specially designed programs for youngsters who use wheelchairs.

Warning. Only after you have the permission of your parents, teacher, or doctor should you make

**IF YOU CAN'T PLAY
—TRY A SWING ANYWAY!**

plans to help your team. If your parents and the doctor decide that some of the duties and drills are not for you, remember that a great many other boys and girls do not play tennis either. You can watch tennis matches on TV or in person. You may even write about the fast action on the court. It's fun to talk about your favorite player or team. You are still a loyal fan even if you cannot be active physically on the team.

15

Rackets Ready!

Every year tennis gains popularity in the United States as more and more people learn about the game.

And year after year, you, your friends, and your family can play a part by being active participants.

Because tennis enjoys great interest worldwide, fans can follow their favorites in action the year round. There is an indoor and outdoor season, with tennis tournaments going on somewhere in the world all year. New fans see the action in person. Many more watch it on TV, listen to it on the radio, and read reports in newspapers and magazines.

In playgrounds, against walls, in backyards, gymnasiums, and parks all over the country, young and old happily play with a tennis racket in their hand. They run, hit groundstrokes, smashes, and volleys.

Whether you are taking part in a tennis tournament or rallying for fun, tennis demands training, conditioning, coordination, timing, speed, a strong heart and breathing system, and an alert mind.

Younger children can improve their early skills in such games as striking a ball, hitting for a target, and chasing a ball to hit it back to the other side.

It's healthy! It's fun! It's exciting for everyone!

Get into the action! Get your tennis racket ready! Move your feet! Hit a drive! Volley! Smash!

Glossary

Ace. A serve that is hit so well that the opponent is unable to touch the ball with the racket for a return.

Advantage. The first point scored after deuce. After each player scores three points, the next point is called advantage. "Ad in" if server scores; "ad out" if receiver scores.

All. When the score is even, or tied. Example is 15–all, 30–all, and so on.

Alley. The court area that lies between the singles sideline and the doubles sideline.

Angle Shot. A ball hit on an angle so it travels across the opposite side of the opponent's court.

Approach Shot. A shot made to allow the hitter to move in toward the net.

Backcourt. The court area between the service line and the base line.

Backhand. A stroke used to hit a ball from the free side of your body. Ball is hit from the left side of a right-handed player and from the right side of a left-handed player.

Ball Person. A boy or girl who chases and returns tennis balls for players during a match.

Base Line. The line at each end of the court. The server must stand behind it when serving the ball. An opponent's ball hit past the base line without bouncing is called "out."

Base Line Game. Game strategy in which players stay near their own base lines and try to win by hitting groundstrokes. The opposite of a "net game," in which players stay near the net.

Bullet. A hard-hit ball that travels with speed.

Cannonball. A hard-hit service ball that travels with speed.

Center Service Line. A line drawn down the center of the court dividing the service courts in half on each side of the net.

Center Strap. A strip of canvas that holds the net in place at the center.

Chip. A short-angled shot made with very little backswing. Often used to make a short slice return of an opponent's serve.

Choke Grip. To take a grip closer to the head of the racket.

Chop. A shot in which the racket is swung sharply downward to give the ball a backspin.

Crosscourt Shot. A shot in which the ball travels diagonally over the net, from one corner of the net to the opposite corner.

Deuce. A tie score, when each player has scored three points, four points, and so on.

Double Fault. Failure by the server to hit either of two consecutive serves into the opponent's service court. The opponent scores a point.

Doubles. A tennis match with two players on a side.

Drive. A forehand or backhand groundstroke that is made from the backcourt and driven deep into the opponent's court.

Drop Shot. A shot hit lightly with so much backspin that it barely clears the net and drops instantly with very little bounce.

Drop Volley. A volley hit with so much backspin that it barely clears the net and bounces very little, just like a drop shot.

Face. The string or surface area of the racket, which is used to stroke the ball.

Fault. A failure to serve the ball into the opponent's service court.

Fifteen. The first point that a player wins in each game.

Flat Shot or Serve. A groundstroke or serve hit without a spin on the ball.

Follow-through. The continued motion of the arm, racket, and body after the ball is hit.

Foot Fault. A violation on the serve when the player stands on the base line or steps onto the playing court before completing the serve.

Forcing Shot. A deep, hard shot made by a player to force the opponent into making an error or weak return.

Forecourt. The area of the court between the net and the service line.

Forehand. A stroke used to hit a ball from the racket side of the body.

Forty. The third point scored by a player in each game.

Game. A portion of a "set," completed by winning four points before the opponent wins three points, or by winning two points in a row after "deuce."

Grand Slam. The winning of tennis's Big Four Championships: the Australian, British, French, and U.S. Nationals.

Groundstrokes. A backhand or forehand stroke made by hitting the ball *after* it bounces.

Half-volley. A stroke used to hit the ball just after it has touched the ground.

Handle. The part of the racket below the frame. The portion between the butt and the frame or head of the racket.

Head of Racket. The strings and frame of the racket, used to strike the ball.

Kill. An overhead smash hit so hard that the opponent cannot return it.

Let. A point to be replayed because of outside interference in a play, or because of a serve that strikes the net but still falls onto the opponent's service court.

Lob. A ball hit so that it travels high over the opponent's head and lands near the base line.

Love. A word used to mean zero or nothing score. Some historians believe the word first came from the French word *l'oeuf*, which means "The egg." When tennis reached England the word was pronounced as "love."

Love Game or Set. You have won a love game when you have not lost a point. You have won a love set when you win six games to your opponent's none.

Match. A contest between two or four players that requires winning two out of three games or three out of five sets.

Match Point. A point which, if won, will allow the player who is ahead in points to win the match.

Mixed Doubles. Doubles competition in which one male and one female play as partners on each side. Examples include a girl and boy team, or daughter and father, wife and husband, and so on.

Net Game. A type of game in which players try to win by reaching a position on the forecourt so that they can make quick volley or overhead shots.

Net Player. A player who likes to move into a position between the service line and the net. In doubles, it's the player who takes a position near the net when the partner is serving.

No Man's Land. The area between the service line and the base line, where players are in a poor position to make their best shots.

Overhead Smash. A hard overhead stroke that is hit

sharply downward onto the opponent's court for a point. Also called a *smash* or *kill*.

Overspin. A ball that spins forward after it is hit. Also called a topspin.

Placing the Ball. Hitting a shot with accuracy to a specific spot on the opponent's court. Usually at a spot where the opponent cannot reach the ball.

Poach. An advanced strategy skill used in doubles play. The net player surprises the opponents by swiftly crossing over to the partner's side of the court to return the ball.

Racket (Tennis). The American spelling of the word "racquet." The older spelling, "racquet," is most often used in England.

Rally. Hitting the ball back and forth across the net either in practice or during a game.

Rankings. At the end of each season players are ranked in order of their playing ability. Players are ranked according to their skill for neighborhood, school, college, national, and world tournaments.

Receiver. The player receiving the serve.

Return. Hitting the ball back onto the opponent's court. Most often refers to a return of the opponent's serve.

Rushing the Net. The action of a player rushing for a position closer to the net after hitting the ball. It is an offensive and aggressive style of play.

Serve or Service. The shot or stroke used by the player (server) to put the ball into play.

Service Break. Occurs when the player serving fails to win a particular game. The receiver "breaks" the other player's serve.

Set. A player must win at least six games to win a set. If each player wins five games, one of the players must win two consecutive games to win the set. A player can win the set by scores of 6–1, 6–2, 6–3, 6–4, 7–5, 8–6, 9–7, and so on. See also Tiebreaker.

Set Point. The very next point, if won by a player who is ahead, that will give that player the winning set.

Singles. Tennis competition in which one player is on each side of the net.

Slice. A groundstroke or volley in which the racket hits downward and forward across the ball to give it a backspin action. Also a serve in which the racket hits across the ball sideways and forward to give it a sidespin action.

Smash. See Overhead Smash.

Spin. A way of hitting a ball that causes it to roll in the air either sideways (sidespin), forward (topspin or overspin), or backward (underspin or backspin).

Tape. A long canvas band that covers the cable or cord at the top of the net.

Thirty. The second point that a player wins in a game.

Throat. The portion of the racket between the head and the grip. It is the part of the handle just below the head of the racket.

Tiebreaker. A method of determining a winner of the set, when set play has reached 6–all, without playing additional games.

Topspin. Hitting the ball up and over the top to give it a forward spin.

Underspin. Hitting the ball down and under the bottom to give it a backward spin.

USTA. The United States Tennis Association, which enforces the rules of championship tennis in the United States.

Volley. A tennis shot in which the ball is hit on the fly before it bounces.

Wood or Frame Shot. A mis-hit ball hit with the frame part of the racket. The shot is considered good if the ball lands in the opponent's court.

INDEX